A Beginner's Guide to Scientific Method

Second Edition

Stephen S. Carey
Portland Community College

Wadsworth Publishing Company
I(T)P® An International Thomson Publishing Company

Belmont, CA • Albany, NY • Bonn • Boston • Cincinnati • Detroit
Johannesburg • London • Madrid • Melbourne • Mexico City • New York
Paris • Singapore • Tokyo • Toronto • Washington

Philosophy Editor: *Peter Adams*

Assistant Editor: *Kerri Abdinoor*

Editorial Assistant: *Kelly Bush*

Marketing Manager: *Dave Garrison*

Production Manager: *Stacey C. Sawyer,
Sawyer & Williams, Incline Village, NV*

Interior Design: *Donna Davis*

Print Buyer: *Stacey Weinberger*

Permissions Editor: *Robert Kauser*

Copy Editor: *Rick Reser*

Cover Design: *Laurie Anderson*

Compositor and Illustrator: *Rogondino &
Associates*

Printer: *Malloy Lithographing*

ISBN 0-534-52843-0

For more information, contact Wadsworth
Publishing Company, 10 Davis Drive, Belmont,
California 94002, or electronically at http://
www.Thomson.com/Wadsworth.html

International Thomson Publishing
Europe
Berkshire House 168-173
High Holborn
London, WC1V 7AA, England

Thomas Nelson Australia
102 Dodds Street
South Melbourne 3205
Victoria, Australia

Nelson Canada
1120 Birchmount Road
Scarborough, Ontario
Canada M1K 5G4

International Thomson Editores
Campos Eliseos 385, Piso 7
Col. Polanco
11560 México D.F. México

International Thomson Publishing GmbH
Königswinterer Strasse 418
53227 Bonn, Germany

International Thomson Publishing Asia
221 Henderson Road
#05–10 Henderson Building
Singapore 0315

International Thomson Publishing Japan
Hirakawacho Kyowa Building, eF
2–2–1 Hirakawacho
Chiyoda-ku, Tokyo 102, Japan

International Thomson Publishing Southern
Africa
Building 18, Constantia Park
240 Old Pretoria Road
Halfway House, 1685 South Africa

 This book is printed on acid-free
recycled paper.

Contents

Preface

This book is written for the student who has little or no background in the sciences. Its aim is to provide a brief, nontechnical introduction to the basic methods underlying all good scientific research. Though I use this book as the main text in a college-level critical thinking course about science and scientific method, it could easily be used as a supplement in any course in which students are required to have some basic understanding of how science is done.

Some will object to the very idea of a basic method underlying all the sciences on the ground that there is probably nothing common to all good science other than being judged good science. While there is certainly something to this objection, I think there are a few basic procedures to which competent scientific research generally adheres in order to be considered good. If anything deserves to be called the scientific method, it is the simple but profoundly fundamental process wherein new ideas are put to the test—ideas from the most rarefied and grand theoretical constructs to the claims of the experimenter to have discovered some new fact about the natural world.

Scientific method rests on the notion that every idea about the workings of nature has consequences and that these consequences provide a basis for testing the idea itself. How this insight is worked out in the world of science is really all this book is about. Certainly much good science is one step removed from the proposing and testing of new ideas, but whenever science attempts to understand how or why things happen as they do, a basic underlying methodology generally emerges. This is not to say that a step-by-step recipe exists that, if followed, will invariably lead to a greater understanding of nature. If I have succeeded at only one thing, I hope it is at showing the tentativeness with which scientific results are issued and the utter openness to revision that is essential to good science.

An essential part of an introduction to anything is an account of what it is not. Hence roughly a third of the text, in parts of Chapter 4 and especially of Chapter 5, is about the antithesis of good science: bogus science or pseudoscience. Explaining how not to do science is all the more important to general students, as much of the presumed "science" to which they will be exposed will be in the form of the rather extravagant claims of the pseudoscientist. To confirm this, one need only turn to any newspaper astrology column or view one of the many television programs that purport to provide an objective investigation of the paranormal.

■

EXERCISES

Students generally learn by doing, not by talking about doing. Thus the student using this text is asked to grapple with every important idea in it by solving exercises. Each chapter ends with a lengthy set of these exercises; they are the parts of the book of which I am most proud and for which I can claim some originality. I have tried to write exercises that are challenging and fun to think about, require no special expertise, and yet illustrate the extent to which scientific problem solving requires a great deal of creativity. Many of the exercises come not from the world of official science but from ordinary life. This illustrates the opening theme of the book: Much of the attempt to do science involves thoroughgoing, hardworking common sense, the very beast instrumental in solving many problems in our day-to-day lives.

Note also two additional features of the exercises. First, they are for the most part written in a manner that requires the student to work with a number of key ideas all at once. At the end of Chapter 3, for example, the student is asked to think about six issues, some of which involve subissues, for each exercise. (Indeed, the exercise instructions are longer than any single exercise!) My preference is to introduce students straight away to the fact that most interesting problems involve a complex of problematic issues and that problem solving begins with two essential steps: (1) getting a good overall sense of the problem or problems and (2) only then beginning to break its solution down into a series of discrete bits of critical work. However, the exercises are designed in such a way that individual tasks can be worked on in relative isolation from one another. So, for example, the first task the student is asked to complete for each of the problems at the end of Chapter 3 is to "state the facts to be explained and the proposed explanation." This task can easily be discussed separately and by reference to each of the exercises.

Second, several of the exercise sets, particularly those at the ends of Chapters 2 and 3, contain many exercises that may seem redundant. I, for one, do not require my students to do every exercise. Rather, I pick a few to use in class for purposes of illustration, and assign a few to be done as homework and then discussed in class. Still others I hold in reserve to deal with particular points that require further discussion, depending on the responses and questions of my students.

The first several exercises in Chapters 2 through 4 all require the student to design some sort of experiment. I have found these exercises particularly useful in encouraging students to think both creatively and critically. I assign different problems to small groups of students as homework to be done as a group. The homework results of each group are then exchanged with another group that must criticize the design submitted by the first group. In class, designers and criticizers meet and refine each of the two experiments on which they have been working. My role in the process is largely to keep the troops calm and to mediate any potentially explosive disputes.

Pedagogical demands aside, I think the appearance of redundancy in the long exercise sets is somewhat superficial. Though in one sense the students are asked to do a few things over and over, in another they are asked to think about very different things in each problem. The contribution of generalized strategies to problem solving, in science and in most other areas of our lives as well, seems to me to be important but not overriding. To solve a problem about X, one may be aided by a general sense of how such problems are solved but one absolutely must know a good deal about X. Thus, the unique considerations—the details—that necessarily intrude in the solution of each problem make that problem worth considering despite the fact that its solution may involve a by now well-worn strategy. The "devil" really is in the details, as can be seen in the sample solutions provided at the end of each chapter.

■
___

NEW TO THE SECOND EDITION

Topical coverage remains the same in this edition though the order in which two major topics are covered has been reversed. In the first edition, the basic procedures involved in testing new ideas were developed first against the backdrop of explanatory claims generally, and then they were applied to the investigation of causal relationships. In this edition, the investigation of causal claims is taken up first. Much of what my students know about science comes to them via media reports on causal research, usually medical research. Thus causation is an ideal topic with which to begin. Moreover, many of the tools needed to deal with other types of research and experimentation are easily introduced using the design of a causal experiment as an exemplar.

Several topics receive a more sustained treatment in this edition and a few are new. In Chapter 2, the notion of a correlation is more completely developed and the statistical jargon is a bit less ponderous. A section has been added to the chapter on how to read and understand media reports about causal research. Chapter 3 now includes a section on functional explanation along with a more detailed treatment of the role auxiliary assumptions play in designing and carrying out tests of explanations. Also included in Chapter 3 is a new set of exercises that challenge the student to distinguish between various types of explanation. Chapter 4 is substantially the same, though now with a slightly longer discussion of descriptions that presuppose a particular explanation. Chapter 5 differs only in containing a more detailed discussion of the ways in which scientific disputes are aired and how mistakes are rectified or, on occasion, overlooked.

I have done some fine tuning in all the exercise sets. There are a few new exercises but the overall number is about the same, save the new exercises mentioned earlier. Finally, you will find interspersed at strategical points what I call *quick reviews*—brief summaries of material from chapter subsections. Their purpose is to provide the text with some breathing room but also to encourage students to stop and reflect on what they have read when they have completed an important topic.

ACKNOWLEDGMENTS

Having taken much credit for some innovation in the writing of the chapter exercises, I can claim little originality for much of the expository material, particularly in the first three chapters. The case study at the center of Chapter 1 will reveal, to those familiar with the philosophy of science, my indebtedness to the work of Carl Hempel, particularly his classic introductory text *Philosophy of Natural Science*. The central approach and organization of Chapter 2 owes much to Ronald Giere's excellent text *Understanding Scientific Reasoning*. I have also had the good fortune to receive the advice of several readers of earlier versions of my manuscript, including Davis Baird, University of South Carolina; Stanley Baronett and Todd Jones, University of Nevada, Las Vegas; Brad Dowden, California State University, Sacramento; Jim Kalat, North Carolina State University; and Bonnie Paller, California State University, Northridge. Special thanks to the reviewers of the first edition, David Conway, University of Missouri, St. Louis; George Gale, University of Missouri, Kansas City; Judy Obaza, King's College; and June Ross, Western Washington University. Nearly every change in the second edition was motivated by their advice and suggestions.

Thanks also go to the reviewers for their helpful comments: David Conway, University of Missouri-St. Louis; George Gale, Jr., University of Missouri-Kansas City; J. A. Obaza, King's College; and June R. P. Ross, Western Washington University.

One final note. Though my field is philosophy, you will find conspicuously missing any emphasis on central topics in the philosophy of science. There is, for example, no explicit discussion of the hypothetical-deductive method or of the covering law model of explanation, nor of their attendant difficulties, nor of the rather more notorious problems in the theory of confirmation, nor of the infighting between realists and antirealists. My hunch is that an introduction to anything should avoid philosophical contemplation about the foundations of that thing, lest it lose focus, if not its course, in the sight of its audience. Once the thing in question is fully absorbed and understood, then and only then is the time for philosophical contemplation of its deep commitments. Though I have not altogether avoided topics dear to the philosopher of science, I discuss them briefly and for the most part in a jargon-free fashion. My hope is that I have not purchased economy and readability at the expense of either accuracy or a sense of wonder about the philosophical issues embedded in the methods by which science is conducted.

Stephen S. Carey

CHAPTER
ONE

Science

JUST WHAT IS SCIENCE?

Science when well digested is nothing but good sense and reason. —Stanislaus

We all have a passing familiarity with the world of science. Rarely does a week go by without a new scientific study or discovery being reported in the media. "Astronomers confirm space structure that's mind-boggling in its immensity" and "Scientists identify gene tied to alcoholism" are the headlines from two recent stories in my daily newspaper. Another story began: "A panel of top scientists has dismissed claims that radiation from electric power lines causes cancer, reproductive disease and behavioral health problems." Yet many of us would be hard pressed to say much more about the nature of science than that it is what scientists do for a living. Hardly an illuminating account!

So what more might we say in response to the question "Just what is science?" We cannot hope to answer by looking at the subject matter of the sciences. Science investigates natural phenomena of every conceivable sort—from the physical to the biological to the social. Scientists study everything from events occurring at the time of the formation of the universe to the stages of human intellectual and emotional development to the migratory patterns of butterflies. Though in what follows we will often refer to "nature" or "the natural world" as being what science investigates, we must understand that the world of the scientist includes much more than our planet and its inhabitants. Judging by its subject matter, then, science is the study of very nearly everything.

Nor can we hope to answer our question by looking at the range of activities in which scientists engage. Scientists theorize about things, organize vast research projects, build equipment, dig up relics, take polls, run experiments on everything from people to protons to plants—the list is almost endless. A description of science in terms of the sorts of things scientists typically do, then, is not going to tell us much about the nature of science for there does not seem to be anything scientists typically do.

If we are to understand just what science is, we must look at it from a different perspective. We must begin by considering why scientists study the natural world.

I

■

ASKING WHY

Of course, we cannot hope to give a simple ubiquitous reason why each and every scientist studies the natural world. There are bound to be as many reasons as there are practicing scientists. Nevertheless, there is a single "why" underlying all scientific research. In general, scientists study the natural world to figure out why things happen as they do. We all know, for example, that the moon is riddled with craters. From a scientific point of view, what is of interest is precisely why this should be so. What natural processes led to the formation of the craters? And so part of the answer to our question "Just what is science?" is: *Science is that activity one underlying aim of which is to further our understanding of why things happen as they do in the natural world.* To see what it is that scientists actually do in attempting to make sense of nature, let's take a look at an historical instance that, as it turned out, played an important role in the development of modern medicine.

Until the middle of the 19th century, little was known about the nature of infectious diseases and the ways they are transmitted. In the mid-1800s, however, an important clue emerged from the work of a Viennese doctor, Ignaz Semmelweis. At the time, many pregnant women who entered Vienna General Hospital died shortly after giving birth. Their deaths were attributed to something called *childbed fever*. Curiously, the death rate from childbed fever in the hospital ward where the patients were treated by physicians was five times higher than in another ward where women were seen only by midwives. Physicians were at a loss to explain why. But then something remarkable occurred: One of Semmelweis's colleagues cut his finger on a scalpel that had been used during an autopsy, within days exhibited symptoms remarkably like those associated with childbed fever, and subsequently died. Semmelweis knew that physicians often spent time with students in the autopsy room prior to visiting their patients in the maternity ward.

Now, the phenomenon that Semmelweis wanted to understand is clear: the remarkable difference in the death rates from childbed fever in the two wards. Owing largely to the clue provided by the death of his colleague, Semmelweis speculated that perhaps childbed fever is caused by something that physicians come into contact with in the autopsy room and then inadvertently transmit to pregnant women during the course of their rounds in the maternity ward. This "something" Semmelweis appropriately termed *cadaveric matter*.

Offering Explanations

In effect, Semmelweis told what for now we might call an *explanatory story*. The story Semmelweis told has two distinct elements. The first are the facts that puzzled him, notably the marked difference in rates of death by childbed fever in the two wards and the fact that physicians attended patients only in the ward where the death rate was higher. The second element is a set of additional but purely conjectural factors that would, if true, account for the difference in death rates. The conjectural factors in Semmelweis's story are the claims that something in cadaveric matter causes childbed fever and that this something can be transmitted from cadaver to physician to patient by simple bodily contact.

As our example suggests, the first step in making sense of some part of nature is to propose an explanatory story that, if true, would explain whatever it is we are trying to understand. Semmelweis's explanatory story is all the more interesting because it introduced notions that were at the time themselves quite new and puzzling: some very new and controversial ideas about the way disease is transmitted. Many of Semmelweis's contemporaries, for example, believed that childbed fever was the result of an epidemic, like the black plague, that somehow infected only pregnant women; others suspected that dietary problems or difficulties in the general care of the women were to blame. Thus with his explanatory story Semmelweis hinted at the existence of a new set of factors that challenged the best explanations of the day and that had the potential to dramatically advance current views about how diseases are spread. However, explanatory stories need not involve controversy. In our daily lives we occasionally work with explanatory stories of a more mundane sort. Thus, to a large extent thinking about things from a scientific perspective—about the "hows" and "whys" of things—involves thinking in ways already familiar to you.

For example, imagine that for the last few nights you haven't been sleeping well. You've had a hard time getting to sleep and have begun waking up frequently during the night. This is unusual, for you are normally a sound sleeper. What could be causing the problem? Well, next week is final exam week and you have been staying up late every evening to study. Could concern about your upcoming exams be causing the problem? This seems unlikely, as you have been through exam week several times before without having sleeping problems. Is there anything else unusual about your behavior the last few nights? It has been quite warm, so you have been consuming large quantities of your favorite drink, iced tea, while studying. And this could explain the problem. For you are well aware that most teas, like coffee, contain the stimulant caffeine, though tea usually contains much less than coffee. It may well be the caffeine in your iced tea that is disturbing your sleep!

Though nothing of any great scientific consequence turns on the solution of this puzzle, the way we undertook its solution nonetheless involves precisely the elements we identified in Semmelweis's work on childbed fever. The puzzling fact here is your recent inability to sleep soundly. The key factors in the explanatory story you have told are your increased iced tea consumption and the fact that iced tea contains a stimulant.

Both of the cases we have examined have something else in common: they provide us with explanations of something puzzling, yet in neither case do we have any tangible evidence that the explanations are correct. Certainly if there is something in cadaveric matter that can cause childbed fever, then Semmelweis's explanation might be on the right track. Similarly, it may be the iced tea that is causing your sleeplessness, but then again it may be something else we have not yet considered. It may even be a combination of the iced tea and other factors. Earlier, we observed that science aims at explaining natural phenomena. Now we need to look at the way proposed explanations are put to the test. Not coincidentally, the second part of the answer to our question "Just what is science?" involves the way explanatory stories are tested both in the world of official science and, as we shall see next, in our daily lives as well.

Testing Explanations

Consider once again our imagined puzzle. You have a hunch that your recent inability to sleep is a result of your increased consumption of caffeine. But is this the right explanation? Here, a relatively quick, easy, and effective test can be performed: drink ice water instead of iced tea in the evening. If you began sleeping normally again it would be a good reason to think that your explanation was right; if not, you might reasonably suspect that caffeine is not the culprit, or at least not the only one.

At the heart of this test lies a three-part strategy. First was looking for a consequence of the explanatory story—that is, something that ought to occur if circumstances were properly arranged and if the story were on the right track: If caffeine is causing your sleeplessness and if you stop consuming it, your sleeplessness ought to stop. Next, you arranged the circumstances: you stopped your caffeine consumption. Finally, you waited to see whether the predicted result would actually occur.

Something very like this same strategy was employed by Semmelweis in testing his explanatory story. He reasoned that if childbed fever is caused by cadaveric matter transmitted from physician to patient, and if something were done to eradicate all traces of cadaveric matter from the physicians prior to their visiting patients in the maternity ward, then the incidence of childbed fever should diminish. So he arranged for physicians to wash their hands and arms in chlorinated lime water—a powerful cleansing agent—before their rounds in the maternity ward. Within two years, the death rate from childbed fever in the ward attended by physicians approached that of the ward attended by midwives. By 1848, Semmelweis was losing not a single woman to childbed fever!

This experimental strategy provides the second part of the answer to our question "Just what is science?" Science is characterized by its underlying interest in making sense of things. It does so first by proposing explanations for natural phenomena, and second by devising experimental conditions under which explanations can be tested. And as we have seen, the experimental strategy on which scientists rely is not all that different from the kind of common sense strategy we ourselves follow in answering the hows and whys of our daily lives.

■

SCIENTIFIC METHOD

You may have noticed that the title of this book is *A Beginner's Guide to Scientific Method*, not *A Beginner's Guide To Science*. What is this thing called scientific method?

If the phrase is used to describe a step-by-step recipe followed by scientists generally in their research, then there is no single scientific method. Our discussion earlier of the broad variety of scientific interests and activities certainly bears this out. But a common thread runs throughout all good scientific research: adherence to the experimental strategy we have been discussing along with a set of basic standards for judging the merits of experiments designed to test explanations. This strategy we can roughly but accurately describe as the basic method of the sciences. In a nutshell, *scientific method is a rigorous process by which new ideas about how some part of the natural world works are put to the test.*

In the chapters to follow we will need to add a great deal of detail to our initial sketch of scientific method. We will also come to recognize that scientific method is not all that straightforward nor, for that matter, easy to apply. Explanations are not always as readily tested as our initial examples might suggest, nor are test results always as decisive as we might like them to be. We shall also find that, with some minor variations, scientific method can be used to test things other than explanations. But when all is said and done, when we have followed the rather intricate twists and turns involved in applying scientific method, we will have at our disposal an accurate picture of the basic methodology underlying scientific research.

The Consequences of Science

Before moving on, an important caveat: In focusing on the preoccupation of science with making sense of nature—with providing and testing explanations—we have ignored what is surely an equally compelling interest of the sciences, namely making the world a better place to live via technological innovation. Indeed, when we think of science we often think of it in terms of some of its more spectacular applications: computers, high-speed trains and jets, nuclear reactors, microwave ovens, new vaccines, and the like. Yet our account of what is involved in science is principally an account of science at the theoretical level, not at the level of application to technological problems.

Don't be misled by our use of the term *theoretical* here. Theories are often thought of as little more than guesses or hunches. In this sense, if we have a theory about something we have at most a kind of baseless conjecture about it. In science, however, *theory* has a related though different meaning. Scientific theories may be tentative and at a certain point in their development may involve a fair amount of guesswork. But what makes them theories is their ability to explain, whether or not they contain questionable notions at some point in their development. Much as there will be tentative, even imprecise, explanations in science, so also will there be secure, well-established explanations. Thus when we distinguish theory from application in science we are contrasting two essential concerns of science: understanding nature and exploiting that theoretical understanding as a means of solving rather more practical technological problems.

It is primarily at the level where new ideas about nature are proposed and tested that science and scientific method fit our description neatly. Yet there is an important, if by now obvious, connection between the worlds of theoretical and applied science. With very few exceptions, technical innovation springs from theoretical understanding. The scientists who designed, built, and tested the first nuclear reactors, for example, depended heavily on a great deal of prior theoretical and experimental work on the structure of the atom and the ways in which atoms of various sorts interact. Similarly, as one of our examples should serve to remind us, simple but effective new procedures for preventing the spread of disease were possible only after the theoretical work of Semmelweis and others began to yield basic insight into the nature of germs and the ways diseases are spread. And, as our other example suggests, even the most mundane applications of scientific method can be of great practical benefit. Anyone who has spent a few restless nights will attest to the significance of getting at the source of the problem.

THINGS TO COME

In the chapters to follow, our central concern is to expand our brief introductory account of scientific method. You will learn a good deal about how to design and assess the results of good scientific tests. Along the way, we will look into what is involved in testing not only explanations but a number of other kinds of claims as well, notably about causes and their effects and about extraordinary abilities. Does secondhand smoke cause lung cancer? Are psychics actually able to bend metal objects by sheer mind power or to discern the thoughts of others? These and lots of other interesting examples will be discussed as we fill in the details of our initial sketch of scientific method.

On our agenda are a number of controversial topics, perhaps none more so than those dealing with the distinction between legitimate and fraudulent applications of scientific method. Nothing can do more to lend an air of credibility to a claim than the suggestion that it has been proven in scientific studies or backed by scientific evidence. Sadly, however, many claims made in the name of science are founded on gross misapplications of some aspect of scientific method. Indeed, so numerous are the ways scientific method can be abused that we find it necessary to devote a chapter to fallacies commonly committed in attempting to marshal scientific evidence for questionable claims.

Our goals, then, in the chapters to follow are twofold. First and most important is to become familiar with the basic methodology common to all good scientific research. Second is to learn to distinguish between legitimate and bogus applications of scientific method. Having accomplished these goals, you should find yourself quite capable of thinking clearly and critically about the claims of scientists and charlatans alike to have advanced our understanding of ourselves and our world.

■

EXERCISES

Try your hand at telling explanatory stories. The following exercises describe curious things. See if you can come up with one or two explanations for each. Keep in mind that your explanations need not be correct but must explain the phenomena if they are true.

1. A recent survey revealed that though 10% of 20-year-olds are left-handed, only about 2% of all 75-year-olds are left-handed.

2. Many baseball players seem to be quite superstitious: Batters and pitchers alike often run through a series of bizarre gestures before every pitch.

3. One of life's little aggravations is the coiled phone cord. No matter how careful we are, it seems phone cords end up horribly twisted.[1]

4. In newspapers, magazines, and books, certain U.S. presidents are referred to by their initials while others are not: FDR, JFK, and LBJ, but not JEC, RWR, GHWB, or WJC.

5. Once in a while, you may find a quarter that has been painted red. Quarters are the only coins painted and, what is more, they are always painted red.

6. If you have ever torn a coupon or article out of a newspaper, you may have noted that when you tear vertically it runs in a straight line, but when you tear across it goes every which way.

Notes

1. Exercises 3–5 are suggested by puzzles discussed in *Why Things Are: Answers to Every Essential Question in Life* by Joel Achenbach (New York: Ballantine, 1991).

CHAPTER

Establishing Causal Links

CAUSES AND EXPLANATIONS

We have said that science aims at furthering our understanding of why things happen as they do. Often this involves getting at the cause or causes of a thing. Why, for example, when we were small children did teeth carefully tucked under our pillows vanish only to be replaced by money? Because while we were sleeping our parents removed them and replaced them with money. Why is there a circular crater several miles in diameter in the Arizona desert? Because a large meteor survived its trip through the earth's atmosphere and crashed to produce the crater. Why is smoking on the increase among young adults? In part because the tobacco industry targets this segment of the population in much of its advertising.

Though explanations can involve notions other than causes—these we will look into in Chapter 3—the investigation of possible causal links is perhaps the most common and fundamental method by which science attempts to advance our understanding of some portion of nature. The causal explanations we have considered so far are all relatively noncontroversial. No one doubts, for example, that a meteor caused the Arizona crater or that parents usually are the culprits when teeth are replaced with money.

But often, causal explanations are proposed about which there may be some real uncertainty. Here are a few claims about potential causal links, all of which have been the subject of considerable scientific interest in the last few years. (1) Recent studies show that the French have much lower rates of heart disease than Americans. One major difference between French and American diets is that the French consume much more red wine. (2) Several years ago, a number of dentists claimed that certain ailments, among them chronic fatigue, were the result of the gradual release into the body of mercury used in dental fillings. (3) Many environmental scientists today contend that chlorofluorocarbons released into the atmosphere are depleting the ozone layer.

8

In all these examples, a claim is made about a possible causal link: in the first, between red wine consumption and heart disease; in the second, between mercury in fillings and chronic fatigue; in the final example, between increased amounts of chlorofluorocarbons in the atmosphere and depletion of the ozone layer. The links are controversial, however, in that though they all have some minimal amount of evidence in their favor it is by no means conclusive. The job of the researcher interested in any of these claims is to try to provide the additional evidence necessary to resolve the controversy. But causal research is often prompted by the discovery of puzzling phenomena, the possible causes of which are simply unknown: (4) Over the last two decades Scholastic Aptitude Test (SAT) scores have decreased significantly nationwide. Why? Suppose we have a hunch that one important factor might be the amount of television students watch. Is television viewing a contributing factor? (5) Psychologists have long suspected that the workplace environment can affect worker productivity. But what specific factors contribute to increased productivity? Imagine we have spent some time observing workers in a large office where productivity has diminished over the past months. At the same time, the company has expanded, with the net effect that the office is clearly overcrowded. Could overcrowding be the cause of decreased productivity?

■
_____

IMPOSING CONTROLS

Examples 1 through 5 all make new and interesting claims about possible causal links. But how do we determine whether such claims are true? Our task in this chapter is to look at the way potential causal links are investigated. The method we will introduce is at the heart of scientific research: the controlled experiment. When one factor is suspected to be a (or the) cause of another, we must arrive at some method to test our suspicions. To this end we must devise a set of circumstances under which we can control for the occurrence of the suspected causal factor. So, returning to one of our examples, if we suspect that overcrowding causes a decrease in productivity, we will want to compare levels of productivity in both crowded and uncrowded conditions—that is, to control for the occurrence of the suspected causal factor: overcrowding.

The notion of a controlled experiment probably brings to mind the image of white-smocked scientists laboring away in the confines of a laboratory. However, this can be misleading. Experiments are indeed often conducted in the rather artificial confines of the laboratory. But experiments take place in the "real" world as well, and may involve the careful observation of natural phenomena or the reactions of subjects in clinical settings, or nothing more than the analysis—the sifting through—of large masses of information. (Experiments, particularly those involving the analysis of information about large groups of people, are sometimes called *studies*. But the distinction between experiment and study is largely a matter of terminology. A carefully controlled study of, say, levels of heart disease and red wine consumption among the populations of several countries constitutes an experiment though it is not conducted in a laboratory and may involve no contact with the experimental subjects!) What scientific experiments have in common— what makes them scientific—is their reliance on some sort of control. To the extent that control can be imposed beyond the confines of the laboratory, controlled experimentation is possible in nearly any setting.

In this chapter we focus on the role controlled experiments play in investigation of possible causal links. The extent to which science in general depends on the notion of experimental control becomes clear as we move on to other topics in Chapters 3 and 4. What we find is that, with some slight modifications, the basic methodology set forth in this chapter guides competent scientific research of just about every sort.

CAUSES AND CORRELATIONS

Before we turn to the question of how causal links are established, we must distinguish between two closely related kinds of claim that frequently occur in discussions of causation. You have probably heard the dictum that "correlation is not causation." More precisely, to establish a correlation between two things is not to establish any sort of causal link between them. A correlation is a statistical comparison between a pair of characteristics. A pair of characteristics are correlated if they display some regular, measurable variance.

The simplest sort of correlation involves the comparison of two groups, one having a given characteristic and the other lacking it. If a second characteristic occurs at different frequencies in the two groups, it is correlated with one of the two. Suppose, for example, that we compare two groups of people between ages 30 and 49. The members of the first group all have completed at least four years of college; those of the second have either no college training or less than four years. Suppose also that we are able to look at the average annual income of the two groups and find that the income of the first group is, on average, 20% higher than that of the second group. This means there is a correlation between education and income in the two groups.

Correlations can be positive or negative. If a characteristic occurs at a greater frequency in one group than in the other, it is positively correlated with the first group; if it occurs at a lesser frequency, the correlation is negative. By contrast, if the characteristic occurs at roughly the same frequency in both groups, there is no correlation between it and either group. In our example, we uncovered a positive correlation between education and income. Suppose instead we had found that the income of those having four or more years of college was actually lower than that of people with less education. This finding would suggest a negative correlation between the two factors. Had we found no real difference in levels of income, we would have had to conclude that, insofar as we can tell, there is no correlation between level of education and income. (This does not mean there is no such correlation, merely that our quick check of the data available does not show one.)

Correlations can also hold between pairs of characteristics within a single group. Within a group, if two measurable characteristics vary in a somewhat regular and predictable fashion, they are correlated. Suppose, for example, we have at our disposal a large amount of information about the freshman class at a small local college. Examining the data, we find what appears to be an interesting relationship between first-semester grade point averages (GPAs) and SAT scores. About 100 students completed the first semester. In most cases, say 75 or so, we find that GPA varies directly with SAT score. That is, if we arrange these 75 students in order of ascending SAT score, we find a corresponding increase in GPAs; the higher the SAT score, the higher the GPA. For the other 25 or so students, we find no regular variance. Some students with relatively high SAT scores have relatively low GPAs and vice versa. Some with average SAT scores have relatively high GPAs, some relatively low. Despite these exceptions, our findings suggest a positive correlation between SAT score and GPA, at least in this group. Had we found just the reverse— that for most students GPA diminished when SAT scores increased—we would have uncovered a negative correlation between SAT score and GPA. Suppose instead we were to discover no regular variance between SAT scores and GPAs—that many students with relatively high SAT scores had average or low GPAs while many with relatively low SAT scores had average or high GPAs. This would suggest that no correlation exists between SAT score and GPA in the freshman class of the college.

As the last example suggests, correlation is seldom an all-or-nothing matter. A perfect correlation between two characteristics would require a one-to-one correspondence between changes in the two. (In our example, increases in SAT score would need to be accompanied by increases in GPA in all 100 cases to establish a perfect correlation.) But particularly when groups of subjects are large, the fact that a correlation is somewhat less than perfect does not undercut its potential significance, perhaps as a predictor of one characteristic in cases where we know something about the quantity of the other. Presuming, in our example, that we have uncovered a fairly consistent positive correlation between SAT score and first-semester GPA, we may be able to predict something about a new college student's chances of success based on his or her SAT score. But here we need to introduce a crucial note of caution: Any inference we draw about an individual based on the evidence of a correlation assumes a causal connection between the correlated characteristics, and this assumption is not always warranted. Remember, correlation is not causation! More precisely, to show that a correlation holds between a pair of characteristics is not to show that the two are causally related.

Why this is so can be seen in the following examples. If we were to examine a group of similar people, say members of a single trade or profession, we could probably unearth a number of correlations. We might find, for example, a correlation between age and income (established either by showing a regular variance between age and income for the whole group or by showing that people above and below a certain age have, on average, different income levels). We would probably also find a correlation between age and the use of reading glasses. Given these correlations, it is likely we will also find a correlation between income and the use of reading glasses! Now, none of these correlations seems to be a coincidence. There seems to be a clear link between age and the need for reading glasses. But the link in the other two cases is much more tenuous; advancing age does not cause one's income level to rise nor does income have any bearing on the need for reading glasses. The link in these two cases is undoubtedly explained by some other factor or series of factors. For example, in most trades or professions the longer one works at a job the more one generally makes. This, then, accounts for the correlation between age and income.

To make matters worse, a correlation may be evidence of nothing more than coincidence, a "mere correlation." This is because unrelated things can vary in regular, measurable ways. For a number of years now, two things have regularly increased: the stock market and the number of minutes per day of television watched by children. Come to think of it, recent increases in the stock market are correlated negatively with a gradual but regular decrease in the number of people who go bowling! And since we are an aging population, probably we could also dredge up a correlation between stock market activity and the sales of reading glasses. These new correlations, of course, suggest nothing more than that lots of things, many of them not causally related, vary over time in somewhat regular ways.

Nevertheless, the search for correlations is an important component of causal research. Indeed, if two things actually are causally linked they will be correlated, so evidence of a correlation may provide some initial reason to suspect two factors are linked. But the simple fact that two things are correlated does not by itself provide evidence of a causal link. To make a case for a causal link between correlated characteristics we would need to establish that the first is responsible for the second or vice versa. And this brings us to our main topic: the method by which experimental controls can be imposed to investigate potential causal links.

■
_____

AN IDEAL TEST

I've invented a new flea collar for dogs; it's made out of organically grown substances—herbs and the like—not synthetic chemicals. I call it the "Nature's Own Way" flea collar, or NOW for short, and I'm sure there is a market for NOW, given current concerns with the environment and utilizing natural substances. But I have one small question that needs to be answered before putting the NOW collars on the market: Do they work? Will my new flea collar actually eliminate fleas? To find out we might perform the following test.

First, we need subjects—a considerable number of dogs of all breeds and all with a considerable number of fleas. So let's borrow, say, 500 experimental subjects from the local humane society. Next we hire a veterinarian and instruct her to screen our 500 subjects, eliminating all but the 200 with the most fleas. Then we divide the

Quick Review: Correlation

- **Positive Correlation**

In two populations, P and Q are positively correlated if a greater percentage of Ps than non-Ps have Q. Suppose that nationwide, people with cell phones have on average a higher income than people without cell phones. Cell phone ownership and income are positively correlated.

In a single population, if a regular increase in one trait, P, is accompanied by a regular increase in another, Q, then the two are positively correlated. Suppose worker productivity at a plant increases as pay increases though with some exceptions. Worker productivity is positively correlated with income.

- **Negative Correlation**

In the two populations, P and Q are negatively correlated if a smaller percentage of Ps than non-Ps have Q. Suppose regular (once a month or more) users of the local public library watch on average much less TV than sporadic or nonusers of the library. TV watching and library use are negatively correlated for the group in question.

In a single population, P and Q are negatively correlated if a regular increase in P is accompanied by a regular decrease in Q. Suppose that the number of visits to the library per month increases as the average number of hours watching TV decreases. Library use and TV watching are negatively correlated.

- **No Correlation**

In two populations, P and Q are not correlated if there is no difference in levels of Q in P and non-P. If equal percentages of males and females are left-handed, there is no correlation between left-handedness and gender.

In a single population, two traits are not correlated if there is no regular variance between the occurrence of the two. Suppose we record both the number of checks written and the number of soft drinks consumed per month by a randomly chosen group of people. We would probably find no evidence that variation in one trait is a predictor of a variation in the other. This suggests there is no correlation between the two.

- **Perfect Correlation**

An invariant relation between two traits; for every change in one trait there is a consistent change in the other. In most species of trees, age in years is perfectly correlated with the number of rings in the tree's trunk; the older the tree the greater the number of rings, without exception.

dogs by assigning each a number, putting the numbers in a hat, and selecting at random two subgroups of 100 dogs each. After isolating the two subgroups from one another, we board them in identical environments. Now comes the crucial step: We put NOW collars on the subjects in the first subgroup but not on those in the second subgroup. After two weeks, we have our veterinarian examine each dog for fleas.

Suppose the results were that all of the dogs in Group 1 are virtually free of fleas while all in Group 2 are riddled with fleas. These results would certainly indicate that NOW collars work—that there is a definite causal link between the use of NOW collars and the eradication of fleas.

What we have just illustrated is the basic strategy followed in designing and carrying out causal experiments—experiments designed to detect causal links. We begin with a claim about a purported causal link, often called a causal hypothesis: "A causes B." Normally, causal hypotheses will be claims about groups, not individuals. In effect, then, "A causes B" really means "A causes B in subjects of type C." The subjects studied in causal experiments will often be people but, as our illustration suggests, can be just about anything. Next we select a limited number of Cs and divide them into two groups of equal size. It is crucial that we select Cs that are alike with respect to any factors, other than A, that we suspect are a cause of B. Our goal is to arrive at two groups of Cs arranged so that if B appears only in one group, the most reasonable explanation is that A is a course of B. The first group is called the *experimental group* (EG), the second the *control group* (CG). The control group is aptly named, for it provides a benchmark for judging whether the level of the effect manifested in the experimental group is actually a product of the suspected causal agent.

Finally, we administer the suspected causal agent, A, to the subjects in EG, but not in CG, and await results. (In the jargon of the causal researcher, the suspected causal agent is sometimes called the *independent variable* and the effect the *dependent variable*.) If after the appropriate amount of time has elapsed only members of EG have B, we conclude that A causes B in Cs. But if the subjects in EG do not have B we conclude that A does not cause B in Cs.

We can set this process out as a series of steps:

1. Begin with a causal hypothesis: A causes B in Cs.

2. Select a representative group of Cs, all of whom are alike with respect to any factor other than A that might cause B.

3. Divide the representative group into two subgroups, the experimental group and the control group.

4. Administer the suspected causal agent A to members of the experimental group only.

5. Wait for the appropriate amount of time.

6. Draw the following conclusions, depending on the results of the test.

    a. If only members of the experimental group have B, the hypothesis is correct: A causes B in Cs.

    b. If members of neither group have B, the hypothesis is wrong: A does not cause B in Cs.

Ideally, a test of this sort provides us with decisive evidence for the truth or falsity of a causal hypothesis. The reason for this should be clear: If we can work with an entirely homogeneous group of experimental and control subjects, and can be certain that in our test the only difference between the two is that the experimental group has been exposed to the suspected cause, then we can be equally certain of our results. If all of our Cs are identical in all relevant respects and if all and only the experimental group of Cs contract B, it would seem A is the cause of B. However, as you are quite aware, we do not live in an ideal world. Though our discussion of an ideal test has provided a sense of what it takes to establish a causal link, it also ignores some very important real-world problems with which causal researchers must contend.

A moment's reflection reveals that even in our imagined experiment, lots of things could happen to render our conclusion questionable. For example, no flea collar is able to eliminate all fleas; furthermore, some breeds of dogs are more susceptible to fleas than others—indeed, particular dogs of a given breed may be more susceptible to fleas than others. Thus in an actual experiment it is unlikely we will be able to achieve either the level of control nor the kind of all-or-nothing results we envisioned in our ideal test. Consider next some of the problems we must confront in carrying out an actual causal experiment.

■
_____

MITIGATING CIRCUMSTANCES

Three important facts about causes and their effects account for most of the difficulties encountered in establishing causal links. First, for most causal factors the level of the effect will be limited, so to say that A causes B in Cs is not to say that all Cs exposed to A will have B. Second, most effects are not associated with a single causal factor; factors other than A may cause B in Cs even when A is clearly a cause of B in Cs. Third, under experimental conditions things other than the suspected causal factor may contribute to the level of effect attributed to the suspected causal factor—that is, A may appear to cause B in Cs when in fact the appearance of the causal link has more to do with the expectations of the experimenters or the experimental subjects than with the introduction of A. Let's consider each of these points, the difficulties they suggest, and ways of dealing with them.

For Most Causal Factors the Level of Effect Will Be Limited

We have all heard the claim that cigarette smoking causes lung cancer. However, this does not mean that all cigarette smokers will contract lung cancer nor even that all who smoke excessively for a long period of time will contract lung cancer. What extensive studies have shown is that more smokers than nonsmokers and more heavy smokers than light smokers will contract lung cancer. In an experiment designed to determine whether A causes B in Cs, we would thus expect to find a difference in the level of B in the experimental and control groups. It would be ideal if we could predict in advance of our experiment precisely the level of difference we expect to get if there is a causal link between A and B. But this is not always possible. When the first studies of smoking and its effects were undertaken, researchers really had no clear idea of what the level of lung cancer in smokers might be. In part, early research was designed just to determine this. However, we can say something in advance of an experiment about the level of difference required to establish that there is a causal link between A and B.

But first we need to discuss a crucial procedure implicit in all causal research: taking samples from large populations. Consider again the claim that A causes B in Cs. If C refers to some large populations, such as human beings or domestic dogs, our experimental and control groups will obviously contain only a minute fraction of the members of our population. Yet the conclusion drawn in a causal study is not to the effect that A does or does not cause B in the Cs we have studied. Rather, the conclusion we will draw is that A does or does not cause B in Cs generally. The reason is that we treat our two groups as samples from the larger population composed of all Cs. So, for example, if a carefully controlled study were to show that 25% of the heavy smokers in the study contracted lung cancer, we would conclude that about 25% of all heavy smokers will contract lung cancer.

The "about" in the last sentence is crucial. Though a properly taken sample can provide us with some sense of what is the case in a larger population, it will normally be only a good approximation. A question we would naturally want to ask about the result just mentioned is: Given that 25% of the sampled smokers contracted lung cancer, just how confident should we be that about 25% of all heavy smokers will contract lung cancer? And how much variance from 25% is close enough to constitute "about" 25%? The answer to these questions is that it depends. More precisely, it depends on the size of our sample. To see the connection between sample size and sample accuracy, consider a simple example.

Imagine we have before us a huge bag we know is filled with thousands of ping-pong balls of two colors, red and blue. We also know that exactly half the balls are blue and half red. Suppose we take a random but very small sample from the bag: two balls. What are the chances that the ratio of blue to red balls in our sample will match the ratio in the bag? Table 2.1, showing all of the possible results, tells us that in exactly half of our possible sampling outcomes (rows 2 and 3), the ratio in our sample will match that in our population. Thus we can say that if we actually took a sample of this size, chances are two in four, 50%, that our sample ratio will match exactly the ratio in the population.

TABLE 2.1

Selection:	#1	#2	Row
	R	R	1
	R	B	2
	B	R	3
	B	B	4

Now, let's expand our sample slightly. Table 2.2 shows the possible results for a sample of four. Note that in Table 2.2 we have four times as many rows as in Table 2.1. This is because we are now considering all possible outcomes from Table 2.1 when selection three is red added to those from Table 2.1 when selection three is blue (rows 1–4 added to rows 5–8). This gives us eight rows and accounts for all possible outcomes for a sample of three balls. To account for selection four, we must double the number of rows for three selections. Thus we must add rows 9–16 to rows 1–8, giving us a total of 16 rows. Rows 1–8 are all the results for three selections when the fourth selection is red: Rows 9–16 are the same three selection results when the fourth selection is blue.

TABLE 2.2

Selection:	#1	#2	#3	#4	Row
	R	R	R	R	1
	R	B	R	R	2
	B	R	R	R	3
	B	B	R	R	4
	R	R	B	R	5
	R	B	B	R	6
	B	R	B	R	7
	B	B	B	R	8
	R	R	R	B	9
	R	B	R	B	10
	B	R	R	B	11
	B	B	R	B	12
	R	R	B	B	13
	R	B	B	B	14
	B	R	B	B	15
	B	B	B	B	16

But something rather curious has happened in our larger sample. First, the chances of getting a sample ratio that matches the ratio in the population have decreased. The ratio in our population, we know, is half red and half blue. But if we count the rows in Table 2.2 that contain exactly two red and two blue balls, we find that only six, or 37.5%, do so (rows 4, 6, 7, 10, 11, and 13). Remember, in our first sample of two, 50% of the possible outcomes matched the ratio in the population. However, in our larger sample something good has happened as well. Though our chances of getting the exact ratio have diminished, the chances of getting a sample ratio close to the ratio in the population have increased! Of 16 rows, 14 contain either one, two, or three red balls (rows 2–15) while only two rows (rows 1 and 16) contain none or four red balls. This, of course, is better than our first, smaller sample, where fully 50% of the possible outcomes contained all or no red balls.

These two samples illustrate an important point about what happens when sample size increases. As the sample grows in size, chances increase of getting a ratio in the sample that is very close to the ratio in the population. Our first, very small sample makes it look as though the chances of exactly matching the population ratio in the sample are greater in small samples. But this holds true only in those special cases where the population ratio matches a possible sample outcome. As we discovered, if the frequency of a characteristic in a population is 50%, we stand a 1-in-2 chance of matching the ratio in a sample consisting of two selections. However, consider what happens to our example if the ratio of blue to red balls in the population is, say, 73% to 27%: No sample of less than 100 can exactly match the population ratio! In general, then, the larger the sample the greater our chances of getting a ratio close to that in the population; however, as sample size increases the chances of getting an exact match between sample and population frequencies decrease.

If, for example, we were to take a sample of 100 from our bag of half red, half blue ping-pong balls, we would find that fully 95% of all possible sample outcomes would contain between 40 and 60 red balls, though only about 8% of the possible outcomes would contain exactly 50. Similarly, if we were to take a sample of 1000 balls, 95% of our possible outcomes would contain between 470 and 530 red balls, though something less than 3% of the possible outcomes would contain exactly 500. Table 2.3 gives similar information for a number of sample sizes taken from a population that, like our bag of ping-pong balls, has a ratio of a given characteristic in the population of exactly 50%—that is, where half the population has the characteristic and half does not.

So, for example, Table 2.3 tells us that if we were to randomly draw 500 balls from our bag, chances are 95% that our sample would contain somewhere between 230 and 270 red (or blue) ping-pong balls. Our choice of the interval containing 95% of all possible outcomes is somewhat though not entirely arbitrary. We could just as easily have settled on another interval, perhaps the one containing 80% of all possible outcomes. Had we done so, we would have found it much narrower than the interval in Table 2.3 with 95% of all possible outcomes. In a sample of 100, for example, 80% of all possible outcomes fall between 43 and 57; for a sample of 1000, between 520 and 580. Note that as we decrease the interval size, the range of

TABLE 2.3

Sample Size	Interval Containing 95% of all Possible Sample Outcomes
25	7–18
50	18–32
100	40–60
250	110–140
500	230–270
1000	470–530
1500	720–780

outcomes under the interval also diminishes, and for a pretty obvious reason: the interval containing 80% of all possible outcomes will have fewer members than the interval containing 95%. Our discussion of sampling has focused on the 95% interval because, as we shall see soon, this is an interval much used in scientific research.

Now, let's reverse our thinking a bit. Suppose that we have before us a huge bag of blue and red ping-pong balls but do not know the ratio of blue to red. So we take a random sample of 1000 balls from it and discover that exactly 500 are red and 500 blue. Table 2.3 tells us that we can be 95% sure that somewhere between 470 and 530 of the balls in the bag are red; had we taken 20 similar samples, we would expect 19 out of 20 of our sample results to fall somewhere between 470 and 530 red balls.

Consider finally a slightly different outcome to our sample. Suppose instead that only 400 balls from our sample turn out to be red. Table 2.3 is not going to help us a lot in figuring out what this ratio means, as it deals only with populations in which the ratio of the characteristic is half and half. Table 2.4, however, adds to the information in Table 2.3 the *margin of error*. Margin of error is nothing more than the interval in Table 2.3 expressed in percentage points, plus or minus, from the ratio in the population.

Table 2.4 gives us an easy but fairly accurate way of determining the reliability of sample outcomes like the one in the example with which we have been working. In a sample of 1000 we found that 400 balls were red. In a sample of this size, the margin of error is roughly +/- 3%. Thus we can be 95% sure that somewhere between 370 and 430 per thousand, or 37% to 43%, are red.

The information given in Table 2.4 can often be applied to media reports of polls and samples. Such reports are often sorely lacking in hard data. But by applying what we have learned so far, we can often draw interesting conclusions even on the basis of somewhat incomplete information. Were we, for example, to read of a poll in which the margin of error is reported to be +/- 4%, we could conclude that about 500 subjects must have been polled. Sometimes reports of margin of error will mention level of significance. This simply refers to the percentage of sample or poll outcomes contained in the "+/-" interval. So a poll based on the margins of error given in

TABLE 2.4

Sample Size	Approximate	Margin of Error*
25		+/-22%
50		+/-14%
100		+/-10%
250		+/-6%
500		+/-4%
1000		+/-3%
1500		+/-2%

* The interval surrounding the actual sample outcome containing 95% of all possible sample outcomes.

Table 2.4 will occasionally be reported as being statistically significant at the .05 level. This is because if 95% of all possible sample outcomes lie within the interval, only 5% lie outside it. Hence in a poll of 500 subjects reported to be statistically significant at the .05 level, chances are only 5% that the population polled will vary by more than 4% from the poll results.

If a sample or poll relies on a smaller interval, say the one containing 80% of all possible outcomes, the margin of error is smaller. But in such a poll we could be only 80% sure that the results reflect the proportion in the population on which the poll was based. Such a result would be reported as statistically significant at the .20 level, as roughly 20% of all possible outcomes lie outside the 80% interval. Similarly, a result reported to be statistically significant at the .01 level would be based on an interval containing 99% of all possible outcomes.

Suppose, for example, that we were to read in the newspaper of a recent political poll reporting that 58% of those polled said they favor a ballot measure to be voted on in an upcoming election. The article also tells us that 500 voters were sampled. From these facts we can draw an interesting and useful conclusion. Following Table 2.4, we can conclude that there is a 95% chance, all things being equal, that somewhere between 54% and 62% of the electorate favor the measure in question. Remember, the margin of error for a sample of 500 is +/- 4%; had the report said only that 58% of those sampled favored the measure and that the result is statistically significant at the .05 level or that the margin or error for this poll is +/- 4%, we could easily determine sample size. By consulting Table 2.4, we would find that the sample must have involved about 500 voters.

A note of caution before we end our discussion of sampling procedures: When the percentages reported in a sample or poll are very high or low, the intervals in Table 2.4 will be off a bit; the range of possible cases on the plus and minus side of the sample outcome will differ slightly from one another. But we need not be too concerned with this minor inaccuracy. The intervals in Table 2.4 are only approximate and intended to provide a rough estimate of the level of precision we can expect from samples or polls of various sizes. Unless sample results are very near to 0% or 100%, the table provides us with a fairly accurate approximation. Had our political poll revealed, for example, that 70% of our 500 sampled voters preferred the measure, the intervals would have been roughly the same.

Earlier we discussed a study claiming that 25% of heavy cigarette smokers sampled contracted lung cancer. The questions we asked about this were: Given that 25% of the sample contracted lung cancer, just how confident should we be that about 25% of all heavy smokers will contract lung cancer? How much variance from 25% is close enough to constitute "about" 25%? It should now be clear that we cannot answer without knowing the size of the sample. Let's assume 1000 heavy smokers were involved in the study. After consulting Table 2.4, we can venture the following answer: there is a 95% chance that somewhere between about 22% and 28% of all similarly heavy smokers in the general population will contract lung cancer. Put in a now familiar way, our interval is statistically significant at the .05 level.

Now that we have a sense of how to estimate the accuracy of samples, we can return to our discussion of causal studies. Earlier we identified a problem: It is not always possible to predict in advance of an experiment the level of the effect we expect to obtain in our experimental group. However, we noted, it should be possible to set some minimal difference in levels of effect between the experimental and control groups that would be sufficient to establish a causal link. We can do this by treating our two groups as samples and working with the margin of error for samples of the appropriate size. Our aim is to determine the amount of difference in the two groups that may be due to chance statistical fluctuations of the sort suggested by our discussion of margin of error. Only differences that have a high probability of being due to something other than chance statistical fluctuation will we regard as indicating a causal link. The minimal level of difference we will set to establish a causal link, then, will be the minimal level that does not have a high probability of being due to sample error.

This will all make more sense if we run through an example. Imagine a causal experiment in which experimental and control groups each contain 100 subjects. At the conclusion of the experiment we find that 42% of the experimental group have the effect we are testing for while only 30% of the control group have the effect. Do we have evidence of a causal link? Look back to Table 2.4.; the margin of error for a sample of 100 is approximately +/- 10%. This tells us two things. First, as 95% of our possible sample outcomes lie within this 20% interval, if we took similar samples 20 times we would expect about 19 of our results to lie within this interval. Second, we can be relatively sure that the characteristic we have sampled for occurs in the population from which the sample is taken at a level somewhere within the 20% interval provided by our margin of error numbers.

But now we need to consider the relationship between two samples, corresponding to our experimental and control groups. In our experiment, 42% of the experimental group had the effect in question. This means that chances are good that in the general population exposed to the suspected causal factor somewhere between 32% and 52% will actually have the effect. In the control group, somewhere between 30%, +/- 10%—that is, between 20% and 40%—will have the effect. Figure 2.1 shows that there is considerable overlap between the two intervals.

FIGURE 2.1

Control Group

20%   40%

Experimental Group

32%   52%

Figure 2.1 tells us that chances are quite high that the difference we have discovered is due to random statistical fluctuations in the sampling process. This does not mean that there is no link between the suspected causal agent and the effect we are testing. One may indeed exist, but the level of effect may be too small to measure using groups of this particular size. We can, however, conclude that this particular experiment has not conclusively established such a link. Were the difference between level of effect in our two groups 20% or more, we would have concluded that the difference is due to something other than the random statistical fluctuations associated with sampling. Quite possibly it is due to the suspected causal factor we are testing.

Had our two groups been larger, the same level of difference would have been significant. Suppose we had worked with experimental and control groups of 500 each. Table 2.4 tells us that the margin of error for samples of this size is +/- 4%. Our intervals would thus look something like the ones in Figure 2.2. As there is a clear gap between the two intervals in Figure 2.2, we conclude that the difference in levels of effect is due to the suspected causal agent.

FIGURE 2.2

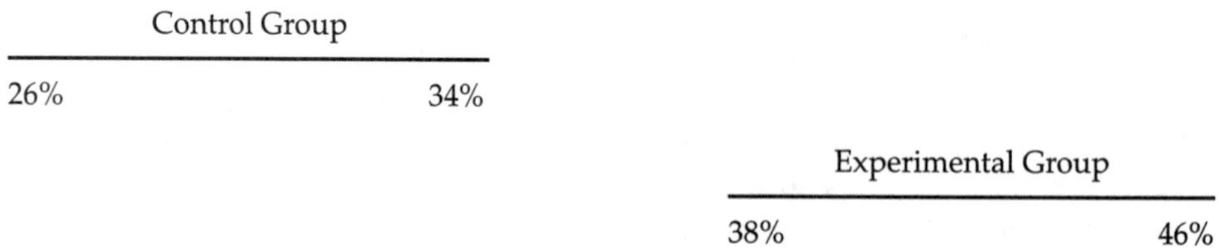

Control Group

26%   34%

Experimental Group

38%   46%

In the jargon of the causal researcher, failure to establish a causal link is often called a *failure to reject the null hypothesis*. The *null hypothesis* is simply the claim that there is no difference between levels of effect in the real populations from which the samples were taken. An experiment that succeeds in establishing a large enough difference in levels of effect between experimental and control groups will often be said to reject the null hypothesis. So in our experiment involving 200 subjects, for example, our results do not enable us to reject the null hypothesis. But in our larger experiment involving 1000 subjects the null hypothesis can be rejected. And this means we have some evidence for a causal link.

Causal experiments do not always involve experimental and control groups of the same size. Even where the groups differ in size, we set minimal levels of difference in much the same way. Suppose, for example, that we have an experimental group of 50 subjects and a control group of 100. In constructing our intervals we need only make sure to work with the proper margins of error, which will be different in each case. Because we are working with percentages we should encounter no difficulty in comparing the intervals.

When the results of causal experiments are reported, researchers often speak of *differences* that are or are not *statistically significant*. Our discussion earlier of statistical significance can guide us in understanding this closely related notion. A difference in the outcome of two samples will be statistically significant when there is no, or at any rate very little, overlap between the confidence intervals for the experimental and control groups. Thus, a difference that is statistically significant is highly unlikely to be due to normal sample fluctuations; chances are slim that two groups, chosen at random, would accidentally differ by the amount we observed in our experiment. Conversely, a result that is not statistically significant suggests there is a great deal of overlap and that the observed difference in levels of effect may well be due to random sample fluctuations.

Reports of statistically significant differences should specify the confidence interval at which the difference is said to be significant. So, for example, a reported difference may be said to be significant at the .05 level. This simply means there is a 95% chance the difference found in the two samples reflects a real difference in the populations from which they were taken. Similarly, a result that is statistically significant at the .10 level is one that stands a 90% chance of reflecting a real difference. Conversely, if we learn that a difference is not statistically significant at the .05 level, we know there is roughly a 95% chance that there is no real difference in the sampled populations; whatever small difference occurred in the two samples is probably due to random statistical fluctuations.

More often than not, causal research uses the .05 level as a benchmark for statistical significance. When this is the case, Table 2.4 can help us to understand the results. But a note of caution: The intervals in Table 2.4 can give us a rough approximation of whether a difference in experimental and control group outcomes is significant, but they are a bit off. The percentage difference required to achieve statistical significance at the .05 level is a bit less than the difference specified in Table 2.4. For example, a difference of just over 13% will be statistically significant for groups of 100 or so. (The required differences decrease even more when levels of the effect are very near to 0% or 100%.) Table 2.4 suggests that a 20% difference would be required. The amount of overestimation in the table decreases as the size of experimental and control groups increases. The table suggests a 6% difference is required to achieve statistical significance for samples of about 1000 when in fact just over a 4% difference will do the trick. We can correct for the inaccuracy in Table

2.4 if we adopt the following rules of thumb in working with reported differences between experimental and control groups:

1. If there is no overlap in the intervals for the two, the difference is statistically significant.

2. If there is some overlap in the intervals (less than one-third of their values in common), the difference is probably statistically significant.

3. If there is a good deal of overlap (more than one-third of values in common), the difference is not statistically significant.

If we keep these points in mind, our method of setting levels of effect and of assessing experimental outcomes will serve us well.

In our discussion so far we have proceeded as though all one needs to design or assess the results of a causal experiment is a good healthy sense of the logic involved in working with samples. But even the most precise and rigorous of statistical analyses fails to address another sort of problem with which we must contend, which brings us to our second point about causes and effects.

Most Effects Are Not Associated with a Single Causal Factor

As a veteran teacher with years and years of experience observing students, I'm convinced that students who attend class regularly generally do better on tests than those who attend sporadically. But personal observation can be misleading; maybe I just remember those good test takers who always came to class because I would like to think my teaching makes some difference. Is there really a causal link between my teaching and the performance of my students? We can determine this by doing a test. I will teach two courses in the same subject next term, each containing 100 students. The only difference between the two will be that in the first attendance will be mandatory, while in the second it will be voluntary. All material to be tested will be covered either in the textbook or in lecture notes to be supplied to all students. Course grades will be based on a single, comprehensive final exam given to all students in both courses.

Suppose now that we have performed this experiment, and at the end of the term we discover a statistically significant difference between the test scores of the two groups. The members of the experimental group—the ones required to attend—score much higher on average than those in the control group, most of whom, by the way, took advantage of the attendance policy and rarely attended class. To ensure accuracy we have excluded the five highest and lowest scores from each group and the average difference remains statistically significant.

Despite the care we have taken in designing our experiment, it nonetheless suffers from a number of shortcomings. Perhaps the most obvious is that it involves no control of factors other than attendance that might influence test scores. One such factor, obviously, is the amount each subject studies outside of class. Remember, tests were based solely on material available to all subjects. What if a much higher percentage of the subjects in the experimental group than in the control group spent considerable time preparing for the final? If this is the case, we would expect the experimental group to do better on the final but for reasons having little to do with class attendance.

The way to avoid this sort of difficulty is by matching within the experimental and control groups for factors other than the suspected cause that may contribute to the level of the effect. Matching involves manipulating subjects in an attempt to ensure that all factors that may contribute to the effect are equally represented in each group. There are several ways of matching. One is simply to make sure that all other contributing factors are equally represented within both groups. This we might accomplish in our experiment by interviewing the students beforehand to determine the average number of hours they study each week. Presuming we can find an accurate way of getting this information, we can then disqualify students from one or the other of our groups until we have equal numbers of good, average, and poor studiers in both groups. Another way of matching is to eliminate all subjects who exhibit a causal factor other than that for which we are testing. Suppose we were to discover that a few students in each group are repeating the course. We might want to remove them altogether from our study.

The final way to match is to include only subjects who exhibit other possible causal factors. We might do this by restricting our study to students all of whom study roughly the same amount each week. If all of our experimental and control subjects have additional factors that contribute to the effect in question, the factor for which we are testing should increase the level of the effect in the experimental group, provided that it is actually a causal factor. Matching in this last way can be problematic if there is any chance that the effect may be caused by a combination of factors. Thus we may end up with an experiment that suggests that A causes B in Cs when in point of fact it is A in combination with some other factor that causes B in Cs.

By matching within our two groups we can frequently account for causal factors other than the one we are investigating. However, there is a way in which unwanted causal factors can creep into an experiment that matching will not prevent. We must be on guard against the possibility that our subjects will themselves determine whether they are experimental or control subjects. Imagine, for example, a student who has enrolled in the course that requires attendance but then hears from a friend about the course that does not require attendance. It seems at least likely that poor students will opt for the course that requires less. Thus we may find that poor students have a better chance of ending up in the control section than in the experimental section. We could, of course, control for this possibility by making sure students do not know the attendance policy prior to enrolling and by allowing no movement from course to course. Another problem we might have here is that poor students in the experimental group, upon hearing of the attendance policy, might drop out, again leaving us with an experimental group not well matched to the control group. In any event, it is worth taking whatever precautions are possible in designing a causal experiment to ensure that subjects do not influence the composition of the experimental and control groups.

Later in this chapter, we look at a number of types of causal experiment and find that, lacking the ability to match and to control for self-selecting samples, many causal experiments lose a great deal of their credibility. So though matching may seem to (and indeed does) involve the artificial manipulation of experimental and control subjects, it is an indispensable tool of the causal researcher.

Experiment Design Factors May Contribute to Effect Level

A may appear to cause B in Cs when in fact the appearance of the causal link has more to do with the expectations of the experimenters or the experimental subjects than with the introduction of A.

Experimenter Expectations Think once again of our test of the role attendance plays in student success. As I am the teacher, it seems only fair that I should be the one to grade the final exams. However, perhaps I will be a bit more lenient, inadvertently or otherwise, in grading the exams of the students in the experimental group. After all, I may have some vested interest in demonstrating my indispensability in the classroom. And if you think about it, my bias here may lead me to teach more effectively to the experimental group than to the control group; in teaching the former group I may spend more time with material that will be on the final exam. One way to avoid the possibility of this sort of bias on the part of experimenters is to insist that they do not know which subjects are in the experimental group or the control group. We might, thus, avoid the former problem by mixing together all 200 final exams prior to my grading them. The latter problem could be solved by having me videotape my class presentations rather than give them in person. Causal experiments in which the experimenter is unaware which subjects are control and which experimental are sometime called *single-blind experiments*.

Experimental Subject Expectations Psychologists have long known that if experimental subjects know they are part of an experiment it can influence their performance. Psychologists call this the *Hawthorne effect*.[1] For example, it is not hard to imagine in our study of attendance and test performance that subjects in the experimental group might work harder if they knew they were part of a group we expect to do well on the final exam. The way to control for the Hawthorne effect in this case would be to make sure students do not know they are taking part in an experiment, at least until it is over. Causal experiments in which subjects are either unaware that they are part of an experiment or do not know whether they are members of the experimental or control groups are another kind of single-blind experiment.

Experiments in which neither experimenter nor experimental subject are aware of which subjects are members of the experimental or control groups are called *double-blind*. Much medical research, for example, is double-blind. Experimental subjects might be given a substance that is thought to prevent a particular condition. Control subjects will often be given a placebo—an inert substance—to control for the possibility of suggestibility; experimenters who work with the subjects and who evaluate the results of the experiment will not be told which subjects are in which groups. The rationale for keeping the experimenter "blind" is to control for the possibility that subjects may be treated differently during the course of the experiment and to ensure that the evaluation of the subject's condition at the conclusion of the experiment will be unbiased.

Quick Review: Questions to Raise in Evaluating the Design or Results of a Causal Experiment

- Has a way been found to control for potential causal factors other than the factor under investigation?

- Is there any way experimenter bias can influence the outcome?

- Is there any way experimental subject expectations can influence the outcome?

- Is any reported difference in levels of effect statistically significant for samples of the size involved in the experiment?

TYPES OF CAUSAL EXPERIMENT

So far in our discussion of causal experiments, we have considered only examples designed by selecting a number of subjects (none of whom have the suspected causal agent), dividing them into two groups, and administering the suspected causal agent to members of one of the two groups. These are called *randomized causal experiments*. But there are two other types of causal experiment, neither of which begin with randomly selected subjects that have not yet been exposed to the suspected causal factor: *prospective* and *retrospective causal experiments* or, as they are often called, causal studies. Prospective and retrospective studies typically provide less evidence of causal links than do randomized experiments but in some situations, for reasons we discuss later, randomized experiments would be difficult if not impossible to undertake. A fourth type of study, the *correlational study*, provides evidence not for a causal link but for a correlation between factors. Following is a brief description of the three basic types of causal experiment and of correlational studies along with a summary of both the advantages and limits of each.

Randomized Causal Experiments

A randomized causal experiment is the very sort of experiment we have been working with. The subjects used in the experiment are selected and randomly divided into two groups prior to administering the suspected causal agent. Randomized experiments are capable of providing strong evidence precisely because they enable us to control quite effectively for other possible causal factors. That subjects are selected prior to being exposed to the suspected cause, coupled with being randomly divided into experimental and control groups, goes a long way toward controlling for extraneous causal factors.

Randomized experiments, however, have a number of disadvantages. They tend to be quite expensive and time-consuming to carry out, particularly if it is necessary to work with large groups of subjects. Unless the suspected effect follows reasonably immediately upon exposure to the causal agent, randomized experiments may take a great deal of time. Does exercise have an influence on longevity? Though we might design a randomized test of the possible link between the two, it would take years to complete. Finally, we would have grave reservations, to say the least, about carrying out randomized experiments dealing with many suspected causal links. Do high rates of cholesterol in the blood cause heart disease? Imagine what a randomized experiment might involve. We might begin, for example, with a large number of small children, divide them at random into two groups, and train one group to eat and drink lots of fatty, starchy, and generally unhealthy foods of the sort we suspect may be associated with high levels of cholesterol. You can see the problem. Not coincidentally, much medical research is carried out on laboratory animals precisely because we tend to have much less hesitation about administering potentially hazardous substances to members of nonhuman species!

Prospective Causal Experiments

In prospective causal experiments we begin with two groups of subjects, one of which—the experimental group—already has the suspected causal factor while the other group does not. During the course of the experiment, we wait to see any emerging level of difference of the effect in the two groups. Consider, for example, how we might carry out a prospective experiment to investigate the link between class attendance and test performance. We might begin by selecting a large number of students at random. Next we must find some way of accurately determining their patterns of class attendance. We might simply observe them for, say, the first ten weeks of my course. Then we divide them into two groups: those who attend class regularly (we might define "regularly" as those who miss less than 5% of all classes) and those who do not. The former become our experimental group and the latter our control group. If we find that more than half of our subjects are in one group or the other, we can pare down the size of the larger group by randomly excluding subjects from it. Now we track them and await the results of the final exam. Such experiments are called prospective because they are future-oriented; they use subjects who already have the suspected cause and wait to see what happens with respect to the effect.

To see the primary limitation of prospective experiments, imagine that we actually carry out the experiment just described and discover a statistically significant difference in levels of test performance between the two groups: the members of the experimental group score much higher on the final on average than the members of the control group. But this may not show a link between attendance and test performance. In selecting individuals for membership in our experimental and control groups we were guided by a single consideration: class attendance. Yet other factors clearly might influence test performance, one of which we discussed earlier: the amount one studies. Undoubtedly there are more, such as how effectively one studies, how motivated one is to achieve outstanding grades, and how much one already knows about the subject matter of the course. By concentrating on a single causal factor in our selection process, we leave open the possibility that whatever difference in levels of effect we observe in our two groups may be due to other factors. This, of course, is precisely where prospective experiments differ from randomized experiments. By randomly dividing subjects into experimental and control groups before administering the suspected cause, we greatly decrease the chance that other factors will account for differences in level of effect. In prospective experiments it is always possible that other factors will come into play, precisely because we begin with subjects already having the suspected cause.

Matching can be used to control for potentially troublesome causal factors in prospective experiments. Suppose, for example, we discover that about 50% of our experimental subjects study five or more hours per week per course but only 35% of our control subjects study at this rate. We can easily subtract some subjects from our experimental group or add some to the control group to achieve similar percentages of this obvious causal factor. It is not an oversimplification to say that the reliability of a prospective experiment is in direct proportion to the degree such matching is successful. Thus in assessing the results of a prospective experiment we need to know what factors have been controlled for via matching. In addition, it is always wise to be on the lookout for other factors that might influence the experiment's outcome yet have not been controlled for. In general, a properly done prospective study can strongly indicate a causal link, though unfortunately not as strongly as can a randomized experiment.

In some respects, prospective experiments offer advantages over randomized causal experiments. For one thing, they require much less direct manipulation of experimental subjects and thus tend to be easier and less expensive to carry out and to occasion fewer ethical objections. Their principle advantage, however, is that they enable us to work with very large groups. And as we have discovered, causal factors often result in differences in level of effect that are so small as to require large samples to detect. Moreover, greater size alone increases the chances that our samples will be representative with respect to other causal factors. This is crucial when an effect is associated with several causal factors. If a number of factors cause B in Cs, we increase our chances of accurately representing the levels of these other factors in our two groups as we increase their size. In addition, prospective experiments allow us to study potential causal links we cannot make the subject of randomized experiments. As pointed out earlier, we would have serious reservations about a randomized experiment dealing with cholesterol and heart disease—in human beings, at any rate. However, we should have no similar moral reservations about a study that involves nothing more than tracking people with preexisting high levels of cholesterol.

Retrospective Causal Experiments

Retrospective experiments or studies begin with two groups, our familiar experimental and control groups, but the two are composed of subjects who do and do not have the effect in question. Remember, in randomized and prospective studies subjects do not have the effect being tested for prior to the beginning of the study. By contrast, retrospective studies look to the past in an attempt to discover differences in the level of potential causal factors.

To carry out a retrospective study of the link between class attendance and test performance, we need only look at records of past classes. We might begin by looking for students who have done well on my final, perhaps those who scored 85% or higher. They become the experimental group; those who scored lower are our control group. Fortunately, I have kept detailed attendance records for all past classes; so we look at them to find our two groups. If there is a link between attendance and test performance we would expect to find significantly better rates of attendance of students in our experimental group.

Even the best of retrospective studies provide only weak evidence for a causal link, because it is exceedingly difficult to control for other potential causal factors. Subjects are selected because they either do or do not have the effect in question, so potential causal factors other than the one tested for may automatically be built into our two groups. A kind of backward matching is possible in retrospective studies. Suppose that in our study of the link between class attendance and test performance we discover that 50% of our experimental group spends five hours or more per week preparing for each of their classes while only 20% of our control group does so. It may be possible to do some matching here by eliminating subjects from one group or adding more to the other and then looking to see if the difference in levels of the suspected cause in the two groups remains the same. However, even if by the process of backward matching we are able to configure our two groups so that they exhibit similar levels of other suspected causes, we have at most very tentative evidence for the causal link in question.

All we are in a position to conclude from a retrospective study is that we have looked into the background of subjects who have a particular effect and found that a suspected cause occurs more frequently than in subjects who do not have the effect. Whether the effect is due to the suspected cause is difficult to say even when pains are taken to control for other potential causal factors, for in manipulating them we may well disturb some combination of responsible factors. That our two groups now appear to be alike with respect to other causal factors is thus largely because they are contrived to appear that way.

One final limitation of retrospective studies is that they provide no way of estimating the level of difference of the effect being studied. The very design of retrospective studies ensures that 100% of the experimental group, but none of the control group, will have the effect. Due to their limitations, retrospective studies are best regarded as a tool for uncovering potential causal links. We discover that a number of people have contracted effect B. Comparing them with a group of people who do not have B, we find a significant difference in the level of some factor A. It would seem that A may well be a cause of B. To determine more about the potential link between A and B, we would be well advised to undertake a more careful prospective or randomized experiment.

The advantages to retrospective studies, in contrast to randomized or prospective studies, are that they can be carried out quickly and inexpensively; they involve little more than careful analysis of data that is already available. And sometimes alacrity is of the essence. Imagine, for example, that we have discovered that Guernsey cows are dying at an alarming rate from unknown causes. Before we can do much of anything, we need some sense of what might be causing the problem. A quick search for factors in the background of infected cows that are absent at a significant level in the background of noninfected cows might turn up just the clue we need.

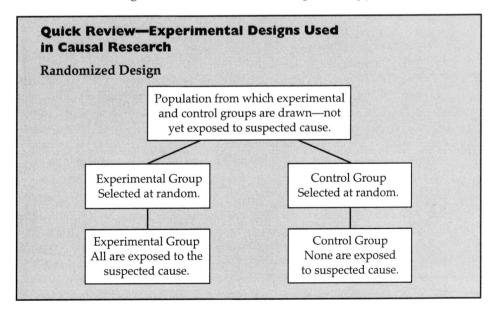

Quick Review—Experimental Designs Used in Causal Research

Randomized Design

Population from which experimental and control groups are drawn—not yet exposed to suspected cause.

Experimental Group Selected at random.

Control Group Selected at random.

Experimental Group All are exposed to the suspected cause.

Control Group None are exposed to suspected cause.

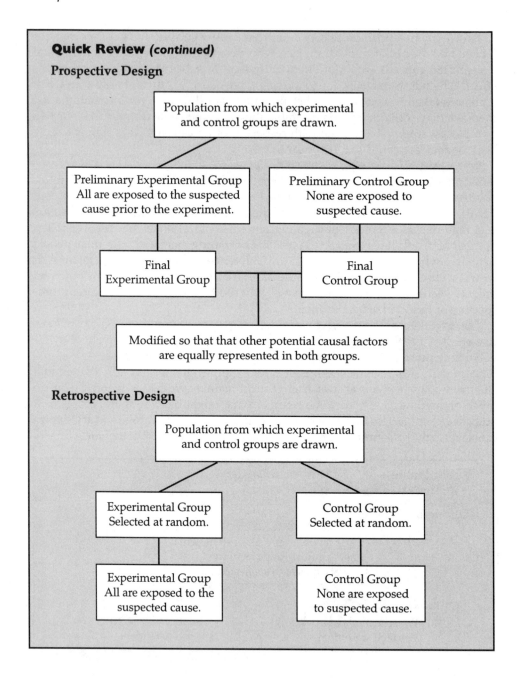

Quick Review *(continued)*

Prospective Design

Population from which experimental and control groups are drawn.

Preliminary Experimental Group
All are exposed to the suspected cause prior to the experiment.

Preliminary Control Group
None are exposed to suspected cause.

Final
Experimental Group

Final
Control Group

Modified so that that other potential causal factors are equally represented in both groups.

Retrospective Design

Population from which experimental and control groups are drawn.

Experimental Group
Selected at random.

Control Group
Selected at random.

Experimental Group
All are exposed to the suspected cause.

Control Group
None are exposed to suspected cause.

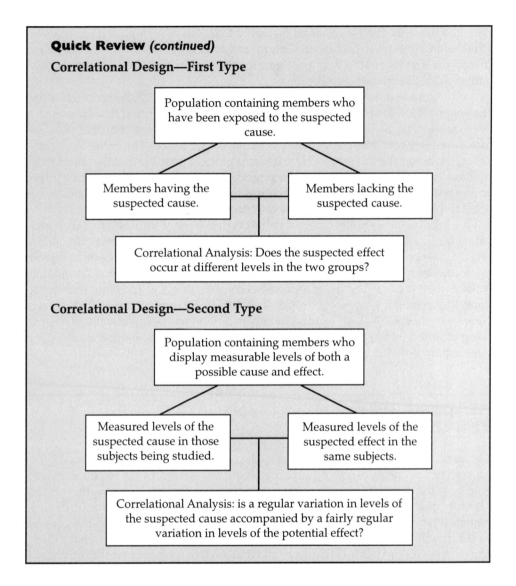

Quick Review *(continued)*
Correlational Design—First Type

Population containing members who have been exposed to the suspected cause.

Members having the suspected cause.

Members lacking the suspected cause.

Correlational Analysis: Does the suspected effect occur at different levels in the two groups?

Correlational Design—Second Type

Population containing members who display measurable levels of both a possible cause and effect.

Measured levels of the suspected cause in those subjects being studied.

Measured levels of the suspected effect in the same subjects.

Correlational Analysis: is a regular variation in levels of the suspected cause accompanied by a fairly regular variation in levels of the potential effect?

Correlational Studies

Earlier we noted that two factors are correlated when they vary in a regular way within a population or when the second factor occurs at different levels in populations having and lacking the first factor. A correlational study is a search, usually within a large statistical base, for interesting relationships between pairs of factors. However, as we pointed out earlier, correlation is not causation. Thus a correlational study alone cannot establish a causal link between the features correlated. Suppose, for example, that we look at the birth dates of students enrolled in my last class and discover that about half were born in one of the first six months of the year. Imagine also that we discover that more than half of all high test scores were achieved by students in this group. This means there is a correlation between being born in the first half of the year and superior test performance. Yet it seems highly unlikely that the relationship is causal.

A stronger candidate for a real causal link might be the following correlation. Suppose we look over the data for several of my courses and find that for roughly three-quarters of all students who have completed them there is a clear positive correlation between test performance and class attendance: The better the attendance, the better the test scores. Here it seems entirely possible that the correlation we have uncovered indicates that attendance may be one important factor influencing test performance. Of course, the question of linkage cannot be settled on the basis of this data alone. Further research is required.

Like retrospective studies, the real value of correlational studies is that they provide a quick and easy way of discovering possible causal links. Absent any additional evidence that a correlation involves a causal link, however, we must regard the results of a correlational study as having established only that: a correlation between two factors. The distinction between causation and correlation is sometimes lost in media reports of correlational studies. Beware of stories that claim a "link," "connection," "tie," or the like between two factors when really all that is being reported on is a correlational study. And this brings us to our final topic for this chapter: popular media reports of causal research.

■
_____

READING BETWEEN THE LINES

The results of causal research are reported in specialized scientific journals. Typically an article includes full information about the design of the experiment, the results, and a complete statistical analysis where appropriate. Conclusions will be carefully qualified and the article will probably contain suggestions for further research. When research uncovers a result that may have an impact on the general public, it will often be reported on in the popular media—newspapers, magazines, and television. And it is in the mass media that most of us encounter the findings of causal research.

Unfortunately, the popular media tend to do a poor job of reporting on the results of causal research. Media reports often leave out crucial information, no doubt in the name of brevity; a 20- or 30-page journal article usually will be covered in a few paragraphs. Such reports tend also to dispatch with the kind of careful qualifications that normally accompany the original write-up of the results. For these reasons, it is important to learn to read between the lines of popular reports if we are to make sense of the research on which they are based.

Here, for example, is the complete text of a newspaper story about an important piece of causal research:

Lithium, which is widely prescribed for manic-depressive disorders, may be the first biologically effective drug treatment for alcoholism, according to studies at St. Luke's Medical Center. The new evidence indicates that the drug appears to have the unique ability to act on the brain to suppress an alcoholic's craving for alcohol. The St. Luke's study involved 84 patients, ranging from 20 to 60 years of age, who had abused alcohol for an average of 17 years. Eighty-eight percent were male. Half the patients were given lithium while the other half took a placebo, a chemically inactive substance. Seventy-five percent of the alcoholics who regularly took their daily lithium pills did not touch a drop of liquor for up to a year and a half during the follow-up phase of the experiment. This abstinence rate is at least 50 percent higher than that achieved by the best alcohol treatment centers one to five years after treatment. Among the alcoholics who did not take their lithium regularly, only 35 percent were still abstinent at the end of 18 months. Among those who stopped taking the drug altogether, all had resumed drinking by the end of six months. (Researchers tested the level of lithium in the blood of the subjects to determine if they were taking the drug regularly.)

Just what are we to make of this story and the research it describes? Is lithium effective in the treatment of alcoholism? (Note that the story begins by claiming that lithium "may be" the first effective treatment for alcoholism.) In trying to make sense of an article like this one, it is necessary to try to answer a number of questions, all based on our findings in this chapter:

What is the causal hypothesis at issue?

What kind of causal experiment is undertaken?

What crucial facts and figures are missing from the report?

Given the information at your disposal, can you think of any major flaws in the design of the experiment?

Given the information available, what conclusion can be drawn about the causal hypothesis?

Let's consider the news article again in light of our five questions.

What is the causal hypothesis at issue?   The hypothesis is that lithium suppresses the alcoholic's craving for alcohol.

What kind of causal experiment is undertaken?   Randomized. Subjects are divided into experimental and control groups prior to the experiment and only the experimental subjects are exposed to the suspected causal agent.

What crucial facts and figures are missing from the report?   The passage gives us no information about what happened to the members of the control group. Nor does it tell us the number of subjects from the experimental group who "regularly took their daily lithium pills." We know that 75% of these subjects did so but this could be as few as three out of four. All we are told of the remaining members of the experimental group is that 35% stayed abstinent and that some stopped taking the drug altogether. We are not told how many are in each of these subgroups. It is possible that the majority of experimental subjects did not remain abstinent. Given the information we have at our disposal, we just cannot say for sure one way or the other. Though we are given no information about the control group, we are provided with some information against which to assess the results in the experimental group: We are told that the 75% abstinence rate is "at least 50% higher than that achieved by the best alcohol treatment centers one to five years after treatment." However, we are not told whether the success rate for treatment centers is a percentage of people who entered treatment or people who completed treatment. If the former is the case, there is a strong possibility treatment centers have a higher rate of success than that established in the experiment. Once again, we can draw no conclusions because we are not provided with the key numbers.

Given the information at your disposal, can you think of any major flaws in the design of the experiment?   One possible flaw comes to mind. It may be that the subjects who continued to take their medication (lithium or placebo) throughout the entire 18 months of the experiment were more strongly motivated to quit drinking than the other subjects. And this may have influenced the outcome of the experiment. Precautions need to be taken to ensure that either no subjects lacked this motivation or else that they were equally represented in experimental and control groups. Here, information about the results of the control group would be helpful. If roughly equal numbers of people dropped out of both groups, we would have some initial reason to think that we had controlled for motivation.

Given the information available, what conclusion can be drawn about the causal hypothesis?   We can conclude very little, particularly because we are given no information about what happened to the control group. This is not to say that the experiment itself warrants no conclusion about the possible link between lithium and alcoholism. However, the report about the study we have been working with has presented us with so little information that we can draw no conclusion.

■

SUMMARY

Let's see if we can reduce our findings about causes and effects and various types of causal experiments to a bare minimum. First, here are brief definitions of some technical terms that come up frequently in discussions of causal experiments:

■ *Causal study*—just another name for a causal experiment.

■ *Causal hypothesis*—just another name for a claim of a causal link.

■ *Controlled experiment*—an experiment in which control is imposed by working with two groups, only one of which has been exposed to a potential causal factor.

■ *Matching*—altering the composition of experimental or control groups to account for causal factors not under investigation.

■ *Null hypothesis*—the claim that there is no difference in levels of effect in the populations corresponding to the two experimental samples.

■ *Single-blind*—an experiment in which either the experimenters or experimental subjects are intentionally deprived of certain information about the experiment, typically about which subjects are in which groups.

■ *Double-blind*—an experiment in which both experimenters and experimental subjects are intentionally deprived of information.

■ *Margin of error*—an interval around a sample outcome wherein a certain percentage of possible sample outcomes lie. In much causal research the interval used contains 95% of all possible sample outcomes.

■ *Statistically significant difference*—a difference in sample outcomes that is highly unlikely to be due to normal sample fluctuations.

Causal experiments are of four distinct types. Here is a brief description of each:

■ *Randomized experiments*—a group of subjects are divided at random into experimental and control groups and the suspected cause is administered to members of the experimental group only.

■ *Prospective experiments*—subjects are selected for the experimental group who have already been exposed to the suspected causal agent; control subjects are selected who have not been exposed to the suspected cause.

■ *Retrospective experiments*—a group of subjects are selected, all of whom have the effect. These subjects are compared to another group in which none of the subjects have the effect in an attempt to discover possible causal factors.

- *Correlational studies*—a population is examined for potential correlations between two factors.

The aim of our first three types of causal experiment is to establish a link between suspected cause and effect. Randomized and prospective experiments attempt to do so by showing that significantly different levels of the effect will occur in two groups, only one of which has been exposed to the suspected causal factor. By contrast, retrospective experiments attempt to establish significantly different levels of the causal factor in groups that do and do not have the effect.

Of our various types of causal experiment, randomized experiments are capable of providing the strongest evidence of a causal link. Retrospective studies provide the weakest level of evidence and are best regarded as a method of discovering possible causal links, not establishing them. Correlational studies do not provide evidence for causal links, but the findings of such a study may suggest areas where further investigation is in order.

In evaluating the design or results of a causal experiment, we must carefully consider each of the following:

1. Is the difference in levels of effect (or levels of cause in retrospective studies) statistically significant for samples of the size involved in the experiment?

2. Have all potential causal factors other than that under investigation been accounted for via matching?

3. Can the possibility of experimenter bias be ruled out?

4. Can effects due to experimental subject expectations be ruled out?

5. Is the experiment clearly designed to provide evidence for a causal link and not just a correlation?

Now it is time to pull everything together. In the exercises that follow you will be asked to design some causal experiments and also to evaluate a number of media reports of the results of causal experiments. The second set of exercises is important because most of the information we get about causal experiments and studies comes to us from television, magazines, and newspapers. Unfortunately, many such reports are woefully incomplete; crucial facts are often missing. However, I think you will find that the information we have covered in this chapter will help you to understand and evaluate studies and experiments reported in the media despite the fact that the reports themselves are often quite sketchy.

■

EXERCISES

Exercises 1–10 all propose causal links. Your job is to design experiments about each of our three types—randomized, prospective, and retrospective—for a proposed causal link. As you go about designing each test, try to criticize your own work. In particular, make sure you are satisfied with the answers to the following questions:

1. *Do you have a good sense, statistically speaking, of the level of effect required to indicate a causal link?*

2. *Have you controlled for other causal factors that might effect the outcome of your experiment?*

3. *Does your experimental design rule out the possibility of experimenter bias?*

4. *Does it rule out effects due to experimental subject expectations?*

(Note: On page 49 a solution is provided for the first problem. Look it over carefully before trying to solve the remaining problems.)

1. Of all people who see chiropractors for lower back problems, 70% report some improvement within 90 days. Is chiropractic manipulation of the spine more effective at treating lower back problems than the methods of treatment employed by mainstream medical doctors? For lower back problems, medical doctors typically prescribe drugs—anti-inflammatories and muscle relaxers—and, in many cases, surgery.

2. Maybe class attendance by itself doesn't have much effect on test performance; a student might attend every class but fail to pay attention to what is going on. And students who pay careful attention to my lectures generally take extensive notes. Thus it seems to me that one factor contributing to high test scores is note-taking. Students who take extensive notes will do better on tests than those who do not.

3. Have you ever had a powerful urge while watching a movie at a theater to purchase popcorn, candy, soft drinks, or the like? No matter how exciting the film, it seems all you can think of is food, food, food. The urge seems to arise even when you are not particularly hungry or thirsty. Though you may not realize it, you may be the victim of subliminal advertising. Here's how it works. When we see a minute's worth of film we actually see nearly 1000 individual frames. Yet consciously we are not aware of any single frame. What some filmmakers allegedly do is insert a single frame every minute or so that contains pictures of various refreshments and a written message like "buy these things now." Even though you are not consciously aware of this message, your subconscious mind may pick it up with the result that you feel a vague urge to purchase the pictured refreshments. The more times you

"see" the message, the stronger the urge becomes. Is it any wonder, then, that we so frequently leave an interesting, compelling film to buy junk food we probably don't even want?

4. Most states now have laws requiring the use of seat belts by automobile drivers. By wearing seat belts, safety experts claim, we reduce the risk of serious injury or death in auto accidents.

5. Many dairy farmers claim that their cows produce more milk when they (the cows) listen to calm, soothing music, the sort we often hear in elevators and shopping malls.

6. Do you find it difficult to concentrate on a test when people around you are talking or moving about? It would seem that auditory and visual distractions reduce our ability to concentrate on a task. But is this so, or do we just use life's normal distractions as an excuse when we perform poorly?

7. Hot colors like red and yellow traditionally have been thought to be mood and activity boosters while cool colors like blue and green are calming. If this is so it would seem that the predominant colors in a workers' environment might have an effect on productivity.

8. We all know that most people cannot perform well under conditions of great stress and that the use of certain psychoactive substances can reduce stress. It would seem to follow, then, that the moderate use of a stress-reducing substance, such as marijuana, will increase a person's ability to perform difficult tasks.

9. Joggers, swimmers, cyclists, and tennis players are always bragging about the benefits of exercise. But are they right? If I exercise regularly, will I increase my chances of living any longer?

10. Clearly, a little encouragement helps us to do better in most things. Could the same be true for plants? If I think positive thoughts about, say, the geranium in my living room when I am tending it, will it do better than if I think negative thoughts?

Exercises 11–25 present reports of causal studies from books, magazines, and newspapers, the very sources on which we base much of what we believe. For each passage, try to answer all these questions:

1. *What is the causal hypothesis at issue?*

2. *What kind of causal experiment is being undertaken?*

3. *What crucial facts and figures are missing from the report?*

4. *Given the information at your disposal, can you think of any major flaws in the design of the experiment and any way of getting around them?*

5. *Given the information available, what conclusion can be drawn about the causal hypothesis?*

(Note: See page 49 for an example of how to solve these problems.)

11. A little exercise can help older people sleep better, researchers reported today in a new study. The study is being published on Wednesday in the *Journal of the American Medical Association*.

    The study, undertaken by researchers at Stanford University, involved 43 sedentary, healthy adults, 50 to 76 years old, with mild to moderate sleep problems, like taking longer than 25 minutes to fall asleep and averaging only six hours of sleep a night.

    Half of those in the study participated in 16 weeks of aerobics, with two hour-long low-impact classes and two 40-minute sessions of brisk walking or stationary cycling each week. The other half did nothing.

    At the end of the study, the subjects who exercised reported that they fell asleep about 15 minutes faster and slept about 45 minutes longer than before. Those who did no exercise showed little or no improvement.

12. Researchers have shown for the first time that nonsmoking adults who grew up in households with smokers have an increased risk of lung cancer. Although 83% of all lung cancer occurs among cigarette smokers, the researchers said their findings suggested that 17% of the cases among nonsmokers result from secondhand tobacco smoke they breathed at home as children.

    The report was written by Dr. Dwight T. Janerich. Janerich's team studied 191 patients who had been diagnosed with lung cancer between 1982 and 1984. The patients had either never smoked more than 100 cigarettes or had smoked at one time but not more than 100 cigarettes in the ten years before the diagnosis of cancer.

    The group was compared with an equal number of people without lung cancer who had never smoked. The researchers added up the number of years each person lived in a house and multiplied it by the number of smokers to calculate smoker years.

    The researchers found that household exposure of 25 or more smoker years during childhood and adolescence doubled the risk of lung cancer. The risk of lung cancer did not appear to increase with household exposure during adult life.

13. In a study convincing enough to jolt any skeptic out of his hammock, investigators at the Institute for Aerobics Research in Dallas have shown that even modest levels of fitness improve survival. Their work began with an objective measurement of fitness of 13,344 healthy men and women of all ages; it ended eight years later with a tally of those who were still alive and those who weren't.

    On entering the study, subjects were asked to keep up with a treadmill programmed to become progressively steeper and faster. Each then received a fitness score. By the end of the study, 283 subjects had died, and a disproportionate number of these had been in the least fit group. The least fit men died at $3\frac{1}{2}$ times the rate of the most fit men. The disparity was even more marked for women; $4\frac{1}{2}$ times. Not only cardiovascular disease but cancer was seen more commonly in the least fit subjects.

    Being above the bottom 20% in fitness level was a big advantage. Further improvement in fitness seemed to have little effect. Couch potatoes take heed: not much exercise is needed to improve the odds by a substantial margin. A brisk walk for half an hour a day will almost certainly suffice.

14. People who overuse a common kind of inhaled medication to relieve asthma attacks face a greatly increased risk of death, a study concludes. The researchers don't know whether the drugs, called beta agonists, are themselves to blame. But they said asthmatics nearly triple their chances of death with each canister of the spray they use each month.

    The research findings were based on insurance records from Saskatchewan, Canada. The study was financed by Boihringer-Ingelheim Pharmaceuticals, a German drug company. The researchers reviewed the records of 129 people who had fatal or nearly fatal asthma attacks. They were compared with 655 asthmatics who had never had life-threatening attacks.

    The study found that fenoterol, a double-strength variety of beta agonist made by Boihringer-Ingelheim, was especially linked to complications. The risk of death increased fivefold with each canister of fenoterol. The study found that the risk of death about doubled with each canister of another variety of beta agonist, called albuterol.

    While use of the drugs was clearly associated with increased risk of death, the doctors could not say for sure that the medicines themselves were to blame. In a statement, Boihringer-Ingelheim noted that people who use beta agonists heavily are also likely to have especially severe asthma.

15. The question: Should you be taking an aspirin every other day as a protection against heart attack? The answer: probably, if you are a man over 40.

    The American Heart Association on Wednesday hailed new research that showed nearly a 50% reduced risk of heart attack in more than 10,000 men taking a 325-milligram buffered aspirin every other day. The physician's Health Study from Harvard University enrolled 22,071 male doctors in two groups. One group took aspirin; the other took a placebo. The researchers report, in this week's *New England Journal of Medicine*, that over four years, the doctors taking aspirin had 47% fewer heart attacks.

Among the 11,037 men who took an aspirin tablet every other day, 99 had nonfatal heart attacks while five had fatal heart attacks. In the placebo group of 11,034 men, there were 171 nonfatal heart attacks and 18 fatal heart attacks during the four years of the study.

16. In a dramatic and controversial finding, a team of psychologists has reported that left-handed people may live an average nine years less than right-handers. The study, which was based on an analysis of death certificates in two California counties, is the first to suggest that the well-documented susceptibility of left-handers to a variety of behavioral and psychological disorders can have a substantial effect on life expectancy.

    Halprin and Coren based their new study on 1000 death certificates randomly selected from two counties in the San Bernardino area of California. In each case they contacted next of kin and asked which hand the deceased favored. All those who did not write, draw, and throw with their right hand were classified as lefties. Someone who wrote with the right hand and threw with the left, for example, was counted as a lefty on the ground that many left-handers were forced long ago to learn to write with the right hand.

    The results shocked the researchers. The average death for the right-handers in the sample was 75 years. For lefties it was 66. Among men, the average age of death was 72.3 for right-handers and 62.3 for left-handers. "The effect was so large it is unlikely to have happened by chance," said Halprin.

17. *The following story appeared roughly two years after publication of the study that is the basis for Exercise 16.*

    Being left-handed is not a hazard to your health after all, says a study that disputes an earlier report suggesting southpaws were at risk of dying up to 14 years sooner than righties.

    Scientists at the National Institutes of Health and Harvard University examined the rates of death among elderly people in East Boston, Mass., and found that left-handed people were at no more risk than right-handed people.

    Dr. Jack M. Guralnik of the National Institute of Aging, a part of the NIH, said the data came from a six-year community study that included 3,774 people 65 or older in East Boston. All deaths were recorded and analyzed.

    Although the study was conducted for other reasons, Guralnik said, the information collected included whether the subjects were left-handed or right-handed. That enabled the researchers to test the theory that southpaws die younger than do right-handed people, he said.

    "Over the six-year period, the death rate was 32.2% among right-handers and 33.8% for left-handers," not a statistically significant difference, Guralnik said. The preferred hand, or laterality, of the people was established by asking which hand was used to write and to cut with scissors. Those who used the right hand were considered right-handers. Those who used the left or either hand were considered left-handers.

Guralnik said 9.1% of the men and 5.8% of the women in the study were left-handed. He said the East Boston study was the most accurate way to find any differences in the rate of deaths between left-handers and right-handers because it compares population groups of the same age. Also, he said, laterality was established by direct interview with the subjects, not by—pardon the expression—secondhand information.

18. In his article entitled "Positive Therapeutic Effects of Intercessory Prayer in a Coronary Care Unit Population," Randolph C. Byrd, M.D., a San Francisco cardiologist, endeavored to answer these questions: (1) Does intercessory prayer (IP) to the Judeo-Christian God have any effect on a CCU patient's medical condition and recovery? (2) How are these effects manifested, if present?

The study took place between August 1982 and May 1983, when 393 patients signed . . . informed-consent papers upon admission to the San Francisco General Hospital CCUA computer-generated list randomly assigned patients to either the IP group or the control group, and neither they nor the CCU doctors and staff nor Randolf Byrd were aware of which patients were assigned to which group.

Intercessors chosen to pray for the IP-group patients were "'born again' Christians (according to the Gospel of John 3:3) with an active Christian life as manifested by daily devotional prayer and active Christian fellowship with a local church." Each IP patient "was assigned to three to seven intercessors. . . . The IP was done outside of the hospital daily until the patient was discharged. . . . Each intercessor was asked to pray daily for a rapid recovery and for prevention of complications and death."

The IP group consisted of 192 patients, and the control group of 201. Analyses revealed no significant statistical differences between the health of the two groups upon admission. "Thus it was concluded that the two groups were statistically inseparable and that results from the analysis of the effects of IP would be valid." The mean age of the IP patients was two years younger than that of the control patients, a difference deemed statistically insignificant.

Each patient's hospital course was given a severity score of "good," "intermediate" or "bad," based upon the degree of morbidity experienced by the patient. In addition, 26 categories of "New Problems, Diagnoses, and Therapeutic Events After Entry" were measured, and tested for statistical significance between the groups. These included such things as congestive heart failure, diuretics, hypotension, intubation/ventilation, pneumonia, and so on.

The results of the study, as reported by Byrd, employing "multivariant [sic] analysis of the data using [these 26] variables . . . revealed a significant difference between the two groups based on events that occurred after entry into the study. Fewer patients in the prayer group required ventilatory support, antibiotics or diuretics." In addition, using the "good/intermediate/bad" severity score, "a bad hospital course was observed in 14% of the prayer group vs. 22% of the controls. . . . chi-square analysis of these data gave a P value of less than .01" (that is, a less than 1% probability that chance alone could account for the difference).

In his introductory abstract . . . Byrd concludes that the "data suggest that IP . . . has a beneficial therapeutic effect in patients admitted to a CCU."[2]

19. In the mid-1970s a team of researchers in Great Britain conducted a rigorously designed large-scale experiment to test the effectiveness of a treatment program that represented "the sort of care which today might be provided by most specialized alcoholism clinics in the Western world."

The subjects were one hundred men who had been referred for alcohol problems to a leading British outpatient program, the Alcoholism Family Clinic of Maudsley Hospital in London. The receiving psychiatrist confirmed that each of the subjects met the following criteria: he was properly referred for alcohol problems, was aged 20 to 65 and married, did not have any progressive or painful physical disease or brain damage or psychotic illness, and lived within a reasonable distance of the clinic (to allow for clinic visits and follow-up home visits by social workers). A statistical randomization procedure was used to divide the subjects into two groups comparable in the severity of their drinking and their occupational status.

For subjects in one group (the "advice group"), the only formal therapeutic activity was one session between the drinker, his wife, and a psychiatrist. The psychiatrist told the couple that the husband was suffering from alcoholism and advised him to abstain from all drink. The psychiatrist also encouraged the couple to attempt to keep their marriage together. There was free-ranging discussion and advice about the personalities and particularities of the situation, but the couple was told that this one session was the only treatment the clinic would provide. They were told in sympathetic and constructive language that the "attainment of the stated goals lay in their hands and could not be taken over by others."

Subjects in the second group (the "treatment group") were offered a year-long program that began with a counseling session, an introduction to Alcoholics Anonymous, and prescriptions for drugs that would make alcohol unpalatable and drugs that would alleviate withdrawal suffering. Each drinker then met with a psychiatrist to work out a continuing outpatient treatment program, while a social worker made a similar plan with the drinker's wife. The ongoing counseling was focused on practical problems in the areas of alcohol abuse, marital relations, and other social or personal difficulties. Drinkers who did not respond well were offered in-patient admissions, with full access to the hospital's wide range of services.

Twelve months after the experiment began, both groups were assessed. No significant differences were found between the two groups. Furthermore, drinkers in the treatment group who stayed with it for the full period did not fare any better than those who dropped out. At the twelve-month point, only eleven of the one hundred drinkers had become abstainers. Another dozen or so still drank but in sufficient moderation to be considered "acceptable" by both husband and wife. Such rates of improvement are not significantly better than those shown in studies of the spontaneous or natural improvement of chronic drinkers not in treatment.[3]

20. Women who took vitamins around the time they got pregnant were much less likely than other women to have babies with birth defects of the brain and spine, a comprehensive study has found. Anencephaly, the absence of major parts of the brain, usually is fatal after a few hours. Spina bifida, the incomplete closing of the bony casing around the spinal cord, typically causes mild to severe paralysis of the lower body. The defects are equally common and strike about 3500 infants each year in the United States, Mulinare said.

     He and his colleagues looked at the data on all babies born with either of the two defects in the five-county Atlanta area from 1969 through 1980. The researchers interviewed mothers of 347 babies born with the defects and 2829 mothers of defect-free babies chosen randomly for comparison.

     The mothers were asked if they had taken vitamins at least three times a week during the three months before they became pregnant and at least three months after conception and if so, what kind of vitamins they took.

     Fourteen percent of all the mothers reported taking multivitamins or their equivalent during the entire six-month period, and 40% overall reported no vitamin use whatsoever. The remainder of the mothers either took vitamins only part of the time or couldn't recall, the researchers said. "We found that women who . . . reported using multivitamins three months prior to conception and in the first three months after conception had a 50% to 60% reduction in risk of having a baby with anencephaly or spina bifida compared with women who reported not having used any vitamins in the same time period," Mulinare said.

     The researchers corrected statistically for differences in the ages of the mothers, their education levels, alcohol use, past unsuccessful pregnancies, spermicide use, smoking habits, and chronic illnesses. All of these factors have been linked to differences in birth defect rates in past research.

21. Women who use hot tubs or saunas during early pregnancy face up to triple the risk of bearing babies with spina bifida or brain defects, a large study has found.

     A report on the study of 22,762 women is published in the *Journal of the American Medical Association*. Of the women studied, 1254 reported hot tub use in early pregnancy and seven of them had babies with neural tube defects, errors in a tube-like structure of cells in the early embryo that eventually develops into the brain and spinal cord. That amounts to a rate of 5.6 defects per 1000 women.

Sauna users numbered 367, of whom two had babies with defects, for a rate of 5.4 per 1000 women. Fever sufferers totaled 1865 women and seven bore babies with defects, for a rate of 3.8 per thousand.

Women with no significant prenatal heat exposure bore defective babies at a rate of 1.8 per thousand.

22 For the first time, a medical treatment has been shown to stop the development of congestive heart failure, a discovery that could benefit 1 million Americans, according to a major study released Monday.

Researchers found that a variety of drugs called ACE inhibitors can prevent—at least temporarily—the start of heart failure symptoms in people diagnosed with damaged hearts.

The five-year study was conducted on 4228 people at 83 hospitals in the United States, Canada, and Belgium. Half the people in the study took enalapril, one form of ACE inhibitor, while the rest took placebos. The study's findings included the following.

Among those getting the ACE inhibitors, 463 developed heart failure, compared with 638 in the comparison group. Taking ACE inhibitors reduced the heart attack rate by 23%.

There were 247 deaths from heart disease in those taking drugs and 282 deaths in the comparison group. This difference, though encouraging, was considered not quite large enough to be statistically meaningful.

The risk of being hospitalized was 36% lower in those persons taking the drug.

23. A large new study produced strong evidence that moderate coffee drinking doesn't increase the risk of heart disease. The study of over 45,000 American men by researchers at Harvard University School of Public Health goes a long way toward exonerating coffee as a heart risk factor.

The researchers queried the men—a group of health professionals—aged 40 to 75 in 1986 about their coffee drinking habits. They followed the men for two years and found that men who drank even as much as three or four cups of coffee a day had no higher risk of developing heart disease than those men who drank no coffee at all.

24. Running and other hard exercise may make many young women temporarily infertile, even though they may think they are able to get pregnant because their menstrual cycles seem completely normal, a new study suggests.

The researchers put young women on a two-month training program and found that only 14% of them had a completely normal menstrual cycle while they were working out. However, the irregularities could frequently be detected only by hormonal tests, meaning some women seemed outwardly to be having regular periods.

The research was conducted on 28 college women with normal menstrual cycles. None of them had ever been in physical training before. They spent eight weeks working out at a summer camp. They started out running four miles a day and gradually worked up to ten miles daily. They also spent three hours a day in other moderately strenuous exercise, such as biking, tennis and volleyball.

Weight loss as well as exercise has been shown to disturb women's reproduction, so in this study, 12 of the women tried to maintain their weight while the rest went on a pound-a-week diet.

Only four of the 28 women had normal periods during the two-month program, and three of those were in the weight maintenance group. The researchers measured sex hormone production that is necessary for women to be fertile and found abnormalities in the release of the hormones were extremely common during exercise, even when the women seemed to be having normal periods. If all had gone routinely, the women would have had 53 menstrual cycles during the exercise program. In 60% of these cycles, there were outward signs of problems, either abnormal bleeding or delayed periods. However, there were hormonal irregularities in 89%. Within six months after the study was over, all of the women had resumed normal menstrual cycles.

25. Smoking more than a pack of cigarettes a day doubles the likelihood a person will develop cataracts, the clouding of the eye lenses that afflicts 3 million Americans, two new studies found.

    The studies, involving almost 70,000 men and women, suggests about 20% of all cataract cases may be attributed to smoking, said a researcher who found a link between the eye disease and smoking in an earlier study. The latest studies involved 17,824 male U.S. physicians tracked from 1982 through 1987 and 50,828 women U.S. nurses tracked from 1980 through 1988.

    In the Physicians' Health Study, subjects who smoked 20 or more cigarettes a day were 2.05 times more likely to be diagnosed with a cataract than subjects who had never smoked, the researchers said. Of the 17,842 men, 1188 smoked 20 or more cigarettes daily, and 59 cataracts developed among them, a rate of 2.5 cataracts per 100 eyes. Among the 9045 men who had never smoked, 228 cataracts developed, a rate of about 1.3 cataracts per 100 eyes. Smokers of fewer than 20 cigarettes daily had no increased risk compared with nonsmokers, the researchers said.

    In the Nurses' Health Study, women who smoked 35 cigarettes or more daily had 1.63 times the likelihood of undergoing cataract surgery as nonsmoking women. The number of nurses in each category was not given. Past smokers of more than 35 cigarettes a day had a similarly elevated risk, even 10 years after they had quit, the researchers found.

    Unlike the doctors' study, the nurses' study showed a proportional increase in cataract risk with amount of cigarettes smoked.

■
_____

A Solution to Exercise I

Look the following solution over carefully. If you spot weaknesses in any of the proposed experiments, try to provide the necessary improvements. Pay particular attention to the various measures taken to control for extraneous factors. As a general rule, it is not a bad idea to ask others to comment on your solutions to the other problems. You may find that a fresh prospective will yield some interesting new ideas to incorporate in your experiments.

The causal link suggested in the problem is between chiropractic treatment (which is left unspecified but generally involves manipulation of the spine) and lower back problems. The question we need to try to answer by our various types of studies is: Is manipulation of the spine more effective at treating lower back problems than is treatment involving drugs and surgery? The passage does not give us the success rate of medical doctors in treating such problems so we want to design experiments that will provide us with information about the relative effectiveness of the two types of treatment.

1. *Randomized experiment.* We might begin with a group of people all having lower back problems of roughly the same severity and none of whom have yet sought medical aid of any sort. Where we might find such a group is difficult to say, but we might cull one from among workers in a profession that is known to involve a high risk of back injury, say furniture movers or longshoremen. Or we might simply run an ad in the newspaper asking for volunteers. At any rate, having found a group of experimental subjects, we will want to "fine tune" the group a bit to account for factors other than treatment known to influence the rate of improvement for back problems: weight, age, and fitness come to mind. Once we have come up with a group of subjects who are pretty much alike with respect to such factors, we will divide them into experimental and control groups.

   Members of the experimental group will be sent to chiropractors for treatment and members of the control group will be sent to medical doctors who specialize in treatment of lower back problems. Since we know that 70% of people who see chiropractors report improvement within 90 days, we need to let our experiment run for at least that long. At the end of the specified period of time, we will evaluate the conditions of the subjects. If chiropractors are more effective than medical doctors we would expect more improvement in the experimental group.

   1a. *Do you have a good sense, statistically speaking, of the level of effect required to indicate a causal link?* The level of difference in effect will depend, of course, on the size of our experimental and control groups. If, say, we were to use two groups of 100, we would expect a difference in levels of effect of about 20% (or perhaps a few percent less), as the margin of error for groups of 100 is +/- 10%. Any smaller difference would warrant the conclusion that the two types of treatment are approximately equal in effectiveness or that any difference in effectiveness is too small to measure in a study of this size.

1b. *Have you controlled for other factors that might affect the outcome of your experiment?* In selecting our initial group we took pains to ensure that all subjects had complaints of roughly the same severity and that all are roughly the same with respect to factors other than those for which we are testing that might contribute to improvement. One other factor comes to mind that might influence our results. There are no doubt differences in the effectiveness of treatment provided by various chiropractors and medical doctors. To control for this, we might want to specify the exact treatments each group will be allowed to use. Beyond this, it is hard to imagine what we might do to further ensure that we have really effective practitioners.

1c. *Does your experimental design rule out the possibility of experimenter bias?* One potential source of bias concerns the experimenter or experimenters who will be evaluating the results. It seems unlikely that most back problems will completely disappear after 90 days, so what will need to be assessed, in many cases, is the level of improvement; one crucial measure of this will be the subjects' subjective reports of how much better they feel—how much less pain they are feeling and how much more mobile they seem to be. Assessing such reports will be difficult enough, since the reports may not be all that precise in any quantifiable way. Here, the preconceptions of the evaluators might influence their rating of various subjects. Hence it seems important that our evaluators not know whether subjects were members of the experimental or control groups.

1d. *Does it rule out effects due to experimental subject expectations?* This question raises a real difficulty for our experiment. We cannot hope to keep our subjects "blind" to the type of treatment they are receiving. And it seems possible that reports by subjects of their level of improvement may be tainted by their beliefs about conventional medical and chiropractic treatment. About the only thing we could do to control for this possibility would be interview our potential subjects prior to the experiment and eliminate those who seem to have a strong bias one way or the other.

One additional factor must be considered in our thinking about this experiment and what various results might be taken to show. As we noted earlier, we have as yet no information about the percent of clients who claim conventional medical treatment is successful for lower back problems. Nor, however, do we know the percent of cases in which such problems improve with no treatment whatsoever! Yet such information would be crucial to the proper assessment of our results. Suppose, for example, we were to discover that chiropractic patients improve at a significantly higher level than do the patients of medical doctors. If the level of improvement for those who seek no treatment is near that of chiropractors, we would need to consider two possibilities: first, that chiropractic treatment is not a causal factor and, second, that medical doctors actually do more harm than good. Fortunately, our results should provide us with some interesting information on this crucial issue.

2. *Prospective experiment.* In a prospective experiment we begin with two groups, one composed of people with lower back problems who are seeking treatment by medical doctors; the other, our experimental group, will be made up of people with lower back problems who are being treated by chiropractors. As our experiment needs only 90 days to run its course, we might admit only people who have started treatment with, say, 10 days to ensure that both groups will be treated over roughly the same amount of time.

   2a. *Do you have a good sense, statistically speaking, of the level of effect required to indicate a causal link?* We may be able to work with larger groups than in our randomized experiment, as we will only need to examine the records of existing patients rather than recruiting a group of potential subjects who fall within a narrow set of guidelines. By beginning with groups much larger than in our randomized experiment, we will be able to accept a much smaller difference in levels of the effect as evidence for a causal link. If, for example, we could work with groups of 500, a difference of only 8% or a little less would suggest that one kind of treatment is more effective than the other.

   2b. *Have you controlled for other factors that might affect the outcome of your experiment?* Many people seek chiropractic care only after conventional medical treatment has failed. Such people may well have problems that are much more difficult to treat than the typical problems for which new back pain sufferers seek treatment. Hence if a large number of chiropractic patients fall into this category we would expect the success rate of chiropractors to be lower than that of medical doctors; a higher percentage of chiropractic patients will suffer from problems that have no quick and easy cure. We might control for this possibility by eliminating from both groups all subjects who have been treated for their back problem by a medical doctor within, say, the last year or so. Another factor that may contribute to the success rates of the two types of practitioners, however, would be difficult to control: Our subjects have chosen the kind of treatment they are undergoing and it seems reasonable to suppose that many of them think the kind of treatment they are undergoing is the most effective. Otherwise they would have selected the other kind. (There are, of course, other reasons why people select chiropractors over doctors and vice versa; one reason why many people select chiropractors—even as their primary physicians—is that chiropractors are typically much less expensive than medical doctors.) Perhaps we can do something about this problem by surveying our subjects and eliminating those with the most outspoken prejudices. A problem with this sort of hands-on treatment of subjects is that it becomes quite time-consuming and expensive when dealing with the large groups that prospective studies have the potential to deliver. Other factors that may affect the outcome of our experiment—such as weight, age, and exercise—can be controlled for by matching.

2c. *Does your experimental design rule out the possibility of experimenter bias?* The same precautions must be taken here as proposed for the randomized experiment discussed earlier. Our evaluators must be kept "blind" about whether subjects were members of the experimental or control group.

2d. *Does it rule out effects due to experimental subject expectations?* Our subjects have, in a sense, determined the group in which they are a member and their choice may well have been influenced by their beliefs about whether chiropractors are more effective that medical doctors. Thus we will want to make sure our subjects do not know the nature of the experiment when they are interviewed at the end of the 90-day test period. Otherwise their evaluation of their own condition may be influenced by their attitudes toward the type of treatment they are receiving.

3. *Retrospective experiment.* In a retrospective experiment, we look into the background of subjects who do and do not have the suspected effect. It may seem that the appropriate study here would be one in which we look for differences in type of treatment for subjects who have reported success after treatment. However, such a study does not meet the requirements for a retrospective experiment in that it involves nothing like a control group. So instead we might compare subjects who have reported improvement after treatment (the experimental group) with subjects who have reported no improvement after treatment (the control group). We can then look for differences in the percentages of people within the two groups who have been treated by chiropractors and medical doctors.

3a. *Do you have a good sense, statistically speaking, of the level of effect required to indicate a causal link?* In retrospective studies there is no way of gauging the level of effect because all subjects in the experimental group will have the effect in question while none in the control group will. We can, however, look for differences in the level of the suspected cause in the two groups. How we do so in this case is a bit tricky. Suppose, for example, we were to discover that among the experimental group 50% were treated by medical doctors, 30% by chiropractors, and 20% by other kinds of practitioners. It may at this point be tempting to conclude that medical doctors have a better success rate. Here lies the value of our control group. Suppose among the control group 70% were treated by medical doctors, 10% by chiropractors, and 20% by others. Suppose also that our two groups each number 1000. Of the 1200 people from the two groups treated by medical doctors (50% of the experimental group plus 70% of the control group), 500 or about 40% reported improvement; of the 400 treated by chiropractors, 75% reported improvement. This would suggest that chiropractors have a significantly higher success rate despite the fact that in our study the raw number of successful treatments for chiropractors is lower than that for medical doctors. Thus it is important to have some sort of control group in order to assess the significance of the results obtained in the experimental group.

3b. *Have you controlled for other factors that might affect the outcome of your experiment?* We might attempt some backward matching. We might, for example, eliminate subjects who have a prior history of treatment if we find that more such subjects visited chiropractors. But such matching provides little additional evidence for any differences we might uncover, as they are adjustments made after the experimental data is in, not prior to the experiment.

3c. *Does your experimental design rule out the possibility of experimenter bias?* The likelihood of experimenter bias seems low in that the experimenters will not have a chance to evaluate individual cases or to determine membership in the experimental or control groups. Attempts at backward matching might be suspect.

3d. *Does it rule out effects due to experimental subject expectations?* Though experimental subject expectations cannot influence the outcome of this experiment, something very similar does come into play. The initial decision as to which group a given subject falls will be completely determined by the subjects' own assessment of their amount of improvement. Moreover, such assessment requires that they compare their current status to their recollection of their condition 90 days or so ago. Such comparisons are liable to involve a lot of guesswork and estimation and to be influenced by the subjects' beliefs about the efficacy of the type of treatment they have undergone.

Notes

1. The *Hawthorne effect* got its name from a series of experiments conducted at the Hawthorne plant of Western Electric Company in Illinois during the 1920s and 1930s. Researchers were interested in isolating factors that might increase productivity, factors like rest periods and lengthened and shortened work days. What they found was that just about any change seemed to increase productivity, leading them to conclude that the Hawthorne effect was in part responsible for the increases: the fact that the workers knew they were being observed led them to work more efficiently. Ironically, a reevaluation of the data from the original experiments many years later suggested the increased productivity of the workers at the Hawthorne plant was not due to the Hawthorne effect! Rather it was due to the fact that the workers had improved their job skills over the months the experiments took place. Though perhaps ill-named, the Hawthorne effect has been well documented in many other experimental settings.

2. Posner, Gary P. "God in the CPU?" *Free Enquiry*, Sprint 1990, Vol. 10, No. 2, pp 44–45.

3. Fingarette, Herbert. *Heavy Drinking: The Myth of Alcoholism as Disease.* Berkeley: University of California Press, 1988.

CHAPTER

THREE

Testing Explanations

■
_____

EXPLANATIONS

Getting at the cause or causes of a thing is one way to explain why it happened. But there are other ways of explaining as well. Why, for example, do our eyelids blink open and shut several times every minute? To keep the surface of the eye moist. Why does a gun "kick" as it is discharged? Because of a well-established physical law: For every action there is an equal and opposite reaction.

Neither of the explanations we have just given involves a cause, at least in any straightforward sense. We normally think of causes as events antecedent to the things they bring about. Physical laws do not cause things to happen in this sense. Nor is the blinking of an eyelid caused by the fact that it thereby keeps the eye moist. As these examples suggest, the notion of an explanation is a bit broader than that of a cause: Though causes provide us with one important sort of explanation, there are other sorts as well.

Our goal in this chapter is to investigate the methods by which explanations generally are put to the test. They are variants on those discussed in Chapter 2. But before we begin looking into the ways explanations are tested we need to do a bit of groundwork. We must first clear away some common misunderstandings about *explanation* as it is used in science and then inventory some of the more prominent types of explanation that occur in scientific research.

Explanation has several distinct senses. When we ask for an explanation, we could be asking for a number of things. If I'm late for an appointment with you, for example, you might ask me to *explain* why I'm late. Here, what you want is my justification—you want to know if I have an excuse for being late. Or to take another example, you might ask your math teacher to *explain* how to solve a particularly nasty problem. Here you are asking to be shown how to do something. But suppose, now, I were to bring to your attention the following rather curious fact: in many states, the letter "O" does not occur on automobile license plates. Your initial thought here might be to wonder why this is so, and you might well ask me to explain. In effect, you are asking neither for the justification of something nor to be shown how to do something but for an account of why something is the case. In what follows, when we speak of an explanation, we are speaking neither of a request for an excuse nor to be shown how to so something. Rather, for our purposes, an explanation is an account of why something happened or continues to happen as it does.

Explanation does not mean *hypothesis* or *theory*. The latter two terms are often associated with explanations in science. Unfortunately, they are used to cover a lot of ground. "Hypothesis" may refer to anything from a vague hunch to a finely detailed conjecture, and more. In Chapter 2 we spoke of *causal hypotheses,* claims about possible causal connections. In general, however, when a claim is characterized as a hypothesis it means that there is something tentative and unproven about it. Thus if I believe there is intelligent life in the universe other than on earth, my belief may be termed a hypothesis because I can produce no hard evidence in its favor. Similarly, untested or suspect explanations are sometimes called *explanatory hypotheses*.

"Theory," though closely associated with the notion of explanation, does not always imply the kind of tentativeness associated with hypotheses. A theory may be a well-developed, well-confirmed body of explanatory material, as in the big bang theory, the theory of evolution, or the germ theory of disease. But often people say things like "That's only a theory," meaning roughly "That's only your opinion of why so and so happened." To make matters worse, many of the things referred to in science as theories are subject to serious question. In astronomy, for example, one highly questionable alternative to the big bang theory is nonetheless referred to as the steady state theory.

The net effect is that when someone speaks of a theory or hypothesis, we may not be entirely clear what they mean. We can avoid any potential confusion in what follows by speaking simply of explanations. Explanations that share with hypotheses a kind of tentativeness we can call *novel* or *proposed* explanations or something similar. Explanations that are well established, like some theories, we may simply characterize as *received, established, generally accepted,* or the like.

New scientific explanations do not arise in an intellectual vacuum; they are occasioned by a desire to make sense of something that puzzles us. This may seem so obvious as to hardly bear remarking. Plainly, if we understand something, there is no sense in attempting to provide it with a novel explanation. Yet two closely related points about the things that puzzle us are worth keeping in mind.

First, we must resist the temptation to think of the puzzling as that which is somehow strange and unfamiliar. Now, puzzling phenomena can indeed be strange and unfamiliar, even spectacularly so. In the late 1980s, for example, hundreds of circular and semicircular indentations were discovered in the wheat and corn fields of southern England. These large, regular patterns were called crop circles, and there seemed to be no obvious explanation for their origin. There was no evidence, for example, that people made the circles; many occurred in the middle of fields where there were no obvious signs of human intrusion.[1] However, much that needs explaining is considerably less mysterious and unfamiliar. The world about us is filled with phenomena with which we are more than passingly familiar, but that we do not know how to explain.

We are all painfully familiar, for example, with many facts about AIDS: how it is transmitted and what its effects are. Yet a great deal remains to be discovered about the nature of the virus and the way it attacks the human immune system. Perhaps nothing is more familiar in our lives than the simple fact that we are creatures capable of thought and feeling. Yet nothing is more puzzling than the way neural-biological processes in the human brain result in mental states, such as those involved in thought and feeling. These examples suggest that both the unusual and the commonplace are ripe for scientific investigation. It has often been remarked that one of the talents of a good scientific researcher is the ability to discern those mundane bits and pieces of our daily lives that if investigated may yield new and important insight on the ways our world works. Also, simply because you or I are puzzled by something does not mean it is genuinely puzzling. Once again, it may seem we are remarking upon the obvious. But as we will discover when we consider the ways explanations are tested, it is not uncommon for people to propose a novel explanation of something because they are unaware that somebody has already adequately explained it.

Rarely, in science, does the need for explanation come to an end. An explanation tells us something about how or why a thing happens, but rarely will it be so complete as to leave no further unanswered "whys" or "hows." For example, we all know that the tides are caused in part by the gravitational attraction of the moon. Thus we can explain the tides by the large amount of water on the surface of the earth, the earth rotating on its axis, and the moon being the source of gravitational attraction and orbiting around the earth. This clearly gives us a sense of why there should be two high and low tides roughly every 24 hours, but it leaves a lot unexplained. What is the process by which gravitating bodies, in this case the moon and the oceans, interact? Put another way, how is it that massive objects such as these have an effect on one another? We might cite here the law of gravity: Objects tend to attract one another in direct proportion to their masses and in inverse proportion to the square of the distance between them. This adds a bit of detail to our explanation, but why should this law hold? Why should objects attract one another at all, let alone in this regular lawlike fashion? Unfortunately, we must leave this unanswered, for little is yet known about what physicists today call the carrier of gravitational interaction, the graviton.

As this example suggests, explaining one thing in science often leads naturally to the need for new, more fundamental explanations. The moral is that in science, at any rate, progress is largely a matter of providing better and better approximations of what is going on in nature. Rarely are explanations final or complete in the sense of leaving no additional unanswered questions.

Scientific progress is not always a matter of supplementing received explanations with more subtle but complementary new explanations. The history of science is fraught with instances where received explanations were supplanted by novel and radically different ones. One of the most well-known examples is the gradual shift from the Ptolemaic concept of the universe to the Copernican.

In the Ptolemaic view, systematized about A.D. 140 by Ptolemy Claudius of Alexandria, the stationary earth stands at the center of the universe and all heavenly objects revolve around it. This view had considerable explanatory power; by a series of complicated calculations the motions of all celestial objects known at the time—the sun, the moon, the five innermost planets, and the stars—could be explained by it, though in ways very different than we would explain them today. For example, careful observation revealed that Mars generally moves eastward across the night sky but occasionally appears to move backward for awhile before resuming its eastward course. In the Ptolemaic view, all celestial objects trace out circular orbits around the earth; Ptolemy explained the backward, or *retrograde*, motion of Mars by introducing the notion of an epicycle—a small circular loop in orbit that from an earthly perspective would make a planet appear to stop and then move backwards. A tribute to its explanatory value is that the Ptolemaic view dominated Western thought for more than a thousand years.

In the 16th century, however, Polish scientist and astronomer Nicolaus Copernicus proposed a new and radically different view of the cosmos. In Copernicus's view, many of the basic assumptions of Ptolemy were wrong: The sun, not the earth, is at the center of things, two planets (Mercury and Venus) occupy orbits nearer the sun than the earth's, and many apparent celestial motions are explained by earth's rotation on its axis. One advantage of the Copernican view is that it suggests a different and simpler explanation for retrograde motion than does that of Ptolemy. If, as Copernicus suggested, the orbit of Mars is outside that of earth, then the apparent double motion of Mars is explained as actually being a single motion that seems double because earth's orbit is inside that of Mars: We observe the motion of Mars from a location that is itself in motion through space such that Mars will on occasion appear to be moving backward even though it is not.

There are a number of interesting facts about this particular episode in the history of science. The first, of course, is the enormous shift in thinking about the nature of celestial motions occasioned by the work of Copernicus. One might think the Copernican "revolution," as it is sometimes called, would have ushered in a new level of accuracy and simplicity in the calculation of planetary motions. But as it turned out, Copernicus's explanation was neither more accurate nor even much simpler than that of Ptolemy. Both views explained roughly the same collection of data about planetary motion. Moreover, like Ptolemy, Copernicus had to introduce a number of epicycles into his work to make his explanation fit the facts. The real value of his achievement, then, resides in the simple but profoundly new way of thinking about celestial motion it introduced.

But our story does not end here. Though in rough outline the Copernican view of the universe finally replaced that of Ptolemy, many details of the former were themselves eventually rejected. Like Ptolemy, for example, Copernicus believed that the planets trace circular orbits around the sun (a conviction that necessitated his introduction of the occasional epicycle in his calculations). It remained for Johannes Kepler to discover nearly a century later that the planets trace out elliptical orbits around the sun. Kepler thereby reduced the kinds of motion required to explain the observed positions of the planets and did away, finally, with the infamous epicycle. In defense of Copernicus and Ptolemy, it must be noted that Kepler had available much more accurate measurements of the movement of the planets than anything available to either of them. Yet despite the enormous import of Kepler's contributions to our understanding of celestial motion, it remained for astronomers long after his time to refine the worldview even further by removing the sun from its exalted position at the center of the universe.

Explanations in science can involve any of a number of distinct sorts of claims. As we have said, an explanation tells us something about how or why an event or series of events happens or happened. To explain something is often to try to get at its cause or causes. But explanations in science often involve a number of other kinds of claim. We can explain by reference to such things as causal mechanisms, laws, and underlying processes, and by specifying the function or role a thing plays in some larger enterprise. As each of these ways of explaining plays an important role in scientific inquiry, we must say a bit about how each is distinctive and how each is related to the others.

Causal Mechanisms

We can know that one thing is the cause of another without fully understanding the causal relationship. There is, for example, strong evidence for a causal link between cigarette smoking and lung cancer. This does not mean that cigarettes are the only causal factor nor that all cigarette smokers will contract lung cancer; still, there can be little doubt that cigarettes are a major cause of lung cancer. Yet despite our confidence in the connection, little is known about the mechanism—the physiological process—by which cigarette smoke leads to uncontrolled cell growth in the lungs of the smoker. In science, explanations often involve claims about causal mechanisms—the processes intervening between cause and effect.

A recent study revealed an apparent causal connection between aspirin consumption and the risk of heart attack. According to the study, men who take a single buffered aspirin every other day have a 50% lower chance of having a heart attack than men who do not. The connection seems fairly well documented. As it turns out, the causal mechanism by which aspirin reduces the risk of heart attack is also well understood: Aspirin interferes with the first stage of the blood-clotting process, and many heart attacks are caused by blood clots in damaged arteries. It seems that when the thin inner wall of an artery is damaged, aspirin inhibits the tendency of minute blood platelets to clot over the damaged area. Thus aspirin reduces the clotting effect that can lead to serious heart attack.

For a very different example more closely related to the use of explanation by causal mechanism in our daily lives, imagine that a friend applies for a job she really wants.[2] Yet now she tells us she finds the job utterly uninteresting and probably won't accept it even if it is offered. Why the change in attitude? We discover subsequently that she learned she had no chance of getting the job. But how, if at all, did this bring about her change in attitude about it? The answer may well lie in a causal mechanism, often called cognitive dissonance reduction, that makes people cease desiring that which they cannot get; you may be familiar with this mechanism under its more common name: sour grapes. Having learned she wouldn't get the job, our friend adjusted her desires to reduce the dissonance caused by wanting something she could not have. No doubt the notion of cognitive dissonance reduction is a bit less precise than the mechanism invoked to explain the connection between aspirin and heart disease, and for that reason would be more difficult to test. But such psychological mechanisms nonetheless play an important role in our attempts at explaining why people behave as they do.

Laws

What happens if heat is applied to a closed container of a gas? Pressure increases. Why? An important law governing the behavior of gases discovered by Joseph-Louis Gay-Lussac answers our question. Gay-Lussac's Law tells us that if the volume of a gas is held constant, the pressure exerted by it varies directly with the temperature. So as we increase the temperature of our gas by applying heat we increase the pressure in the closed container. Such laws explain by revealing how particular events are instances of more general regularities in nature.

A law is universal when it claims that a particular kind of behavior will occur in all (or no) cases. Thus Gay-Lussac's Law is universal: it makes a claim about the behavior of all gases. But scientific laws need not be universal; some claim only that a particular kind of behavior will occur in a certain proportion of cases.

Suppose we were to learn that a good friend, a nurse, has contracted hepatitis B. We are aware that he works in a clinical setting where patients with hepatitis B are regularly treated. We are also aware that recent studies have shown that an alarmingly high number of health care workers contract the hepatitis virus from their clients—one of four who are accidentally exposed to the virus will actually contract it.[3] It seems a real possibility that our friend's condition is explained in part by the statistic just cited. The explanation we might give would go something like this:

> Exposed health care workers have a 25% chance of contracting hepatitis B. Friend F is a nurse who works in a setting where the risk of exposure to hepatitis B is high. F has hepatitis B. Thus, it is likely F contracted hepatitis B from a client.

Here we have an example of explanation by law but where the law is not universal. Remember, a universal law tells us that a particular kind of behavior will occur in all cases. Yet our law says that only 25% of exposed health care workers, not all of them, will contract the virus.

No doubt it seems odd to call this claim a law, yet it is certainly lawlike just as Gay-Lussac's law is lawlike; both describe a regular correspondence. In the case of Gay-Lussac's law the correspondence is between the pressure, volume, and temperature of a gas, and in the case of our latter law the correspondence is between workers who are exposed to the virus and those who subsequently contract hepatitis B. The difference is that laws of the latter sort, often called *statistical laws*, give explanations that must be carefully qualified. It may be that our friend has contracted the hepatitis virus from someone or something other than a client and, as our statistical law tells us, chances are quite good that exposure to clients with the virus will not lead to infection. Thus, we had to qualify our explanation by adding the phrase, "it is likely," to acknowledge the possibility that our explanation may be wrong for this particular case.

Underlying Processes

You are probably aware that fluorescent lamps are much more efficient than traditional incandescent bulbs. The explanation lies in the way each produces light. When light is produced by incandescent bulbs, electrical energy passes through a wire, heating it until it incandesces (glows). The wire, called a filament, typically is made of a metal called tungsten; the enclosing bulb around the filament directs or diffuses the light. The problem is that 90% of the energy put into such a bulb is released in the form of heat while only 10% results in light. Fluorescent lamps produce light in a different way, by energizing gas. Electrical energy flows into electrodes at the ends of a tube. The electrodes emit electrons, which energize a small amount of mercury vapor held at very low temperatures inside the tube. The energized mercury molecules radiate ultraviolet light, which is in turn absorbed by a phosphorescent coating on the inside of the surface of the tube, thus producing visible light. This process produces very little heat; fluorescent lamps are able to convert almost 90% of the energy they consume into light. So the amount of electrical energy required by a fluorescent lamp to produce a given amount of light is substantially less than that required by incandescent bulbs.

This explanation accounts for an observable phenomenon—the greater efficiency of fluorescent lights—by making reference to the process underlying the phenomenon being explained. Our explanation involves electrons, electrodes, filaments, and gases and the way electrons behave under various conditions. In effect, we have explained one process by reference to a detailed description of what is occurring at a more fundamental level of the same process.

Explanation by reference to underlying processes is quite common in science and something very much like it occurs in daily life as well. Suppose, for example, you discover a leaky faucet in your kitchen. You turn the faucet handle to the "off" position, but water continues to drip. So, having first turned off the water supply to the sink, you proceed to take the faucet apart and discover that one of the washers inside the shutoff valve is worn out. The explanation of the leaky faucet—the worn out washer—involves a process that, in a sense, underlies the observed phenomena.

Function

We often explain the things we and others do (and don't do!) by reference to our hopes, wants, aspirations, beliefs, and the like. "Why," I might ask, "are you only having a salad for lunch?" "Because," you might explain, "I want to lose a few pounds." To explain one thing by reference to the purpose it fulfills is to give a functional explanation. So to explain our behavior by reference to what we hope to achieve, as in this example, is to give one sort of functional explanation. Human behavior is not the only thing susceptible to explanation by reference to function or purpose. If you asked me about the rock sitting on my desk, I would explain that a heating duct is located just over my desk that blows unsecured papers about whenever the heat comes on, so I use the rock as a paperweight. Following a similar strategy, we might explain that a carburetor is the component of an internal combustion engine that mixes fuel and oxygen. In both of these examples, we explain by specifying the purpose the thing in question serves. The purpose of the rock on my desk is to hold down papers; the purpose of a carburetor is to mix fuel and oxygen.

In the social sciences, functional explanation plays a central role. An historian or economist, for example, might explain the emergence of a social practice—say, slavery or liberalized abortion laws—by reference to the role such practices play in some larger social or economic enterprise. Slavery, it seems, was instrumental in the development of economies of scale in the 18th-century United States. Liberalized abortion laws adopted in the 1960s reflected changing attitudes about the role of women in society and thus provided women greater latitude in making decisions about their future.

As the examples suggest, functional explanations often make reference to the purpose or purposes of the thing being explained. Because of this, it may seem that functional explanation will be useful in dealing only with human contrivances and behavior. But functional explanations can provide insight into other sorts of cases as well, cases in which "purpose" implies nothing about human intervention, planning, or forethought. For example, functional explanations are often used in the biological sciences. One of the most influential figures in the scientific revolution was the British physician William Harvey (1578–1657). Perhaps Harvey's greatest accomplishment was his discovery that the purpose of the heart is to act as a sort of pump, facilitating the circulation of the blood. Similarly, evolutionary biologists often explain the dominance of a trait within a species on the basis of the advantage it confers on those that have the trait—that is, on the purpose it serves.

But in such cases, "purpose" need not be understood on the model of human purposes. As used in biological explanations it means something more like "role in some larger enterprise." To give the purpose is to specify that role. So, for example, to wonder about the purpose served by the bright colors of many species of flowers is merely to consider how this trait is beneficial in their propagation. Bees, it seems, are attracted to brightly colored flowers and thus bright coloration tends to enhance the chances of pollination. In a perfectly harmless sense, then, the purpose of bright coloration in some flower species is to attract potential pollinators. But in this sense, to explain by reference to the purpose served by a trait is not to suggest anything like the underlying intelligence we associate with human purposes.

More than one type of explanatory claim may be involved in a chain of explanations. Earlier we noted that in science the need for explanation rarely comes to an end. This fact is reflected in the interdependence of the various types of explanation we have just considered. Knowing, for example, that the function of a carburetor is to mix fuel and oxygen, we might then go on to consider how a carburetor accomplishes this goal. And here we will probably need something like an explanation of underlying processes. We will, in other words, need to consider how a carburetor's parts operate in conjunction with one another to accomplish the proper mixture of fuel and oxygen. A sense of the function something performs thus can often guide our understanding of how and why the thing operates as it does. (This strategy is sometimes called *reverse engineering:* Figure out what a thing is intended to do, then consider how it is designed and built to accomplish that end.)

Or, to take another kind of case, if we want to understand more about a particular causal connection we will need to speculate about causal mechanisms that may be involved. For example, if a lake is polluted and some of its indigenous species of wildlife begin to diminish, there seems to be a connection. But what is the process by which greater pollution leads to less and less wildlife?

Similarly, if we want to understand more about why a lawlike regularity obtains, we may need to consider underlying processes. Recall our discussion earlier of Gay-Lussac's Law: If volume is held constant, the pressure exerted by a gas varies directly with the temperature. Why, we might wonder, should this particular relationship between temperature, volume, and pressure hold for gases? The answer requires that we examine the processes underlying the phenomena described by our gas law. Gases are composed of molecules rushing hither and thither at enormous speeds. Pressure on the container holding the gas is a result of gas molecules colliding with the walls of the container. When heat is applied to the container, it is translated into increased activity on the part of the molecules of gas. The result is that the number of collisions with the container increases, thereby increasing the pressure exerted on the container by the gas. (This is a very rough sketch of a basic notion in what is called the kinetic theory of gases.)

Or if we want to understand more about a process underlying something we may need to look once again for causal mechanisms and lawlike regularities, considerably more fine-grained in character. To return for a moment to our story about the process involved in fluorescent lighting, why would mercury molecules, bombarded by electrons, radiate ultraviolet light? To answer we need to consider processes that intervene and perhaps even underlie the interaction of electrons and mercury molecules.

You may well wonder whether the process of explaining can ever come to an end and, if so, when. These are deep and profoundly difficult philosophical issues. Some philosophers speculate that as a given science matures, claims about causal connections and mechanisms will be replaced gradually by broader and broader laws describing more and more causal phenomena. In this view, the most fundamental kind of scientific understanding is that provided when laws are discovered that reveal something about the interconnectedness of a wide variety of phenomena; the wider the variety, the greater the understanding. Other philosophers maintain that at least in certain sorts of cases, perhaps all, to explain a thing is to identify its immediate cause or causes and that when we can find no further intervening mechanism, the process of explanation must come to an end. In this view, lawlike statements, no matter how broad and unifying, merely help us classify and describe the rather more basic causal process at work in nature. For our purposes, however, we need not wrestle with these deep philosophical issues. Suffice it to say, the kind of explanatory claim one will give—whether it be about causes, causal mechanisms, laws, underlying processes, or something else—will depend on how much one knows and, of course, what one wants to explain.

Many explanations do not need to be tested. Consider again a puzzle discussed earlier: the rather curious fact that, in many states, the letter "O" is not used on license plates. Let me propose explanation E:

> Most states also use numbers on their license plates and the letter "O" could easily be confused with the numeral "0." Thus the letter "O" is not used to avoid possible ambiguities in recording and reporting license plate numbers.

E seems to clear up the puzzle—if E is true. And there seems to be no obvious reason to think that E is not true. Certainly E squares with what we know about the kind of concern that might prompt a large bureaucracy to adopt this sort of policy: the need to be able to assign unique, unambiguous identification codes to large numbers of vehicles, people, and other items. No doubt we could verify E by making a few phone calls to the appropriate government agencies, but there would be little point in doing so, absent any reason to suppose E false.

By contrast, we would want to find some independent means of verifying an explanation when there is some substantial question as to its correctness. Now, we may question an explanation because we have some reason to believe it false. But more often our interest in a novel explanation will be prompted simply because though it fits the facts and would if true account for the phenomenon at issue, we just have no other reason to believe it true. Lately, for example, I have noticed that I have a much harder time reading small print as the day wears on. It occurs to me that my eyes may tire more easily now than when I was younger. Is fatigue the right explanation? Given what little I know about physiology and the aging process, my explanation seems to make some sense and it certainly fits the facts. But I confess I have no idea whether it is actually correct. Thus my explanation is an ideal candidate for testing. Aside from the fact that it would, if true, account for my reading problems, is there any independent reason to think fatigue is the correct explanation? The point of testing a novel explanation like this one is to try to arrive at an answer to this question.

■

PRELIMINARY REQUIREMENTS

Before testing a novel explanation we must satisfy ourselves that two crucial requirements are met. First, there should be no question of the accuracy of the description of the phenomenon to be explained. Second, there should be no noncon-

Quick Review: Ways of Explaining

■ **Causes**

To explain one thing or event by reference to another, antecedent thing or event. Examples: "Debris from last night's windstorm caused the power outage." "Excessive alcohol consumption can damage the liver."

■ **Causal Mechanisms**

To explain by citing intervening causal factors that explain the effects of a more distant cause. Example: "Debris from the storm severed several power lines, thus causing last night's power outage."

■ **Laws**

To explain an event by referring to a general law or principle of which the event is an instance. Examples: "The fuel efficiency of a vehicle is determined in part by size and weight. This is because acceleration is directly proportional to force but inversely proportional to mass. Thus the larger the object you want to move, the greater the force you need to apply and the more energy you need to expend." "Auto insurance rates are higher for teenagers because as a group they tend to be involved in more accidents and also because insurance companies base rates in part on information about group driving behavior."

■ **Underlying Processes**

To explain something by reference to the workings of its component parts. Example: "The chest pain and breathing difficulty symptomatic of pneumonia results from an infection of the lung tissue. The tiny air sacs of which the lungs are composed, called alveoli, fill with inflammatory fluid caused by the infection. As a result, the flow of oxygen through the alveolar walls is greatly impaired."

■ **Function**

To explain something by reference to the role it fulfills in some larger enterprise. Examples: "Many species of birds build their nests in high places—trees, cliffs, and the like—to protect their young from predators." "The lungs serve both as a means of introducing oxygen into and removing carbon dioxide from the bloodstream."

troversial explanation available that accounts for the puzzling phenomenon—that is, one like E that both clears up the puzzle and is itself highly plausible—that we have independent reason to suppose true or, at any rate, no reason to doubt. So crucial are these two preliminary requirements that we need to consider each in more detail before turning to the question of what is involved in testing novel explanations.

Do we have an accurate description of the phenomena to be explained? Many people claim that strange things happen when the moon is full. One interesting and curious claim is that more babies are born on days when the moon is full or nearly full than during any other time of the month. Why do you suppose this is so? Is there something to astrology after all? Do the moon and the planets have an effect on our lives? Is it the gravitational pull of the moon tugging at the embryonic fluid surrounding the unborn child? Before beginning to speculate in this fashion about possible explanations, we would do well to back up a step. If it is true that more births occur near a full moon than at other times, we have a genuine mystery. But is it true? Careful studies done at a number of hospitals strongly suggest that it is not. When birth rates were examined over the period of a year or two, it turned out that on average there were no more or fewer births during the period near a full moon than during any other period. In a given month, there might be a few more (or less) births then than during other parts of the month, but when averaged out over a long period of time the difference disappears, and with it the need for explanatory speculation.

As it turns out, then, what is most interesting about this case has little to do with the puzzling phenomena we were led to consider but rather why people might believe in a phenomenon despite clear evidence to the contrary. The answer lies in a common mistake people make in marshaling support for generalizations they believe to be true. This mistake is called *confirmation bias*. In supporting a general claim—such as "more births occur when the moon is full than at other times"—it is easy to look inadvertently at data that support the claim while ignoring data that suggest it may be false. Suppose, for example, you and I work in a hospital maternity ward. We have both heard the claim in question and are aware that a number of our colleagues believe it. Under these conditions it would be all too easy for us to think back and recollect only those of our experiences that tend to confirm the general proposition that more births occur when the moon is full.

Indeed, it would be difficult not to do this; our tendency is to recall experiences that are unusual or singular in their significance. I doubt, for example, that you can recall what you were doing on, say, February 8 last year though I am confident you can recall something of what you did on the day you graduated from high school.

The selectivity with which we remember, coupled with our tendency to look for evidence that confirms things we already believe to be so, suggests that we should approach most generalizations with a certain amount of caution. We should be particularly skeptical of generalizations about the unusual and puzzling, like our claim above about the moon and birth rates. Our initial impulse in such cases should be to consider the nature of the evidence for the claim. Close inspection of the evidence may reveal that something that initially appears to be puzzling is, after all, not so.

Most of us have had the disconcerting experience of receiving a phone call or visit from someone just as we were thinking of them. Is some sort of mental telepathy involved here? Such experiences seem unusual and mysterious only if we fail to put them in perspective by considering the enormous number of times we have thought of some person or other but have not received a phone call or visit from them soon thereafter. Given the number of times some person or other enters our thoughts, it seem entirely unremarkable that on occasion we will be contacted by a person we have been thinking about recently. If we think such events are evidence that something puzzling and not understood is going on, we are probably guilty of confirmation bias in concentrating on just those few events that confirm the possibility of mental telepathy.

Not that puzzling phenomena cannot be securely established. Suppose, for example, that the studies mentioned earlier about birth rates and the full moon had uncovered evidence that there are significantly more births when the moon is full than at other times. Then we would have a genuine mystery on our hands. The point is that before accepting such a conclusion we should insist on the sort of evidence provided by careful long-term observation that can correct for confirmation bias and the natural selectivity with which we remember.

Are more plausible rival explanations available? Imagine that you are unable to find your keys. You have searched all morning to no avail and you know they should be around the house somewhere because you remember using them to open the door when you came home late last night. One possible explanation is that you've simply put them somewhere that you haven't looked yet. But other explanations are available as well. Perhaps someone who shares the house with you has inadvertently taken your keys instead of theirs. These two explanations rival one another in that both, if true, would serve to explain the phenomena in question. Presumably, at least one of the two is wrong, though in just the right circumstances I suppose they might both be correct.

What makes one explanation more plausible than its rivals is a bit more difficult to say. Let's begin by considering a couple of explanations for your missing keys that are a bit more bizarre than the two we have considered so far. Perhaps someone broke into your house while you were asleep and stole them. Or perhaps they just disappeared into thin air. Stranger things have been known to happen! Compare these two new explanations with the first one we proposed, that you simply misplaced your keys. It seems at least fairly plausible, as it makes no reference to other things that themselves would need to be explained. Surely you've misplaced things before only to have them turn up even after you were convinced they were lost forever.

Consider next the first of our rather more bizarre explanations: Somebody stole your keys. Keep in mind here, the point of an explanation is to make sense of how or why something has happened. If in giving an explanation we invoke things that are themselves quite puzzling, we have really only avoided the question of why the event happened. Why would someone break into your house and only take your keys? And why is there no evidence of forced entry? Though I suppose these things could be explained—maybe we are dealing with an incredibly clever and skilled burglar who intends to return when you are not home—I think you can see that each additional explanation makes the original explanation seem less and less likely. A whole string of events would have to occur in order for our second explanation to remain plausible, but our final explanation does no good at all. The keys just disappeared into thin air? How does this work? Were they consumed by a tiny black hole? Did they spontaneously melt? A simple puzzle has now involved us in great mysteries.

In the jargon of the scientist, our two bizarre explanations violate *Ockham's razor,*[4] a principle named after its author, medieval philosopher and monk William of Ockham (1285–1349). Ockham's own version is somewhat obscure: "What can be done with fewer is done in vain with more." A more appropriate version of this principle for our purposes is the following: Given competing explanations, the truth of any of which would explain a given puzzle, we should initially opt for the explanation that itself contains the least number of puzzling notions. The rationale behind this admonition should be clear. If a puzzle can be explained without introducing any additional puzzling notions, there is no good reason to entertain an explanation that does.

By comparison with our two bizarre explanations, the explanation that you put your keys somewhere you haven't looked yet fits the bill here. So to say that one of a series of rival explanations is the most plausible is to say it is the one most in keeping with Ockham's razor. Keep in mind that Ockham's razor does not rule out explanations that involve notions not fully understood. It only suggests that given competing explanations, we should favor the one that involves the least number of problematic notions. Forced to choose between clever burglars and black holes to account for the missing keys, Ockham's razor would suggest the former.

Interestingly enough, under the right circumstances we could appeal to Ockham's razor to help us think about our first two explanations for the missing keys. Suppose, for example, that your roommate rarely if ever takes things belonging to you, inadvertently or otherwise. Suppose also that you constantly misplace things. Under these circumstances Ockham's razor would suggest favoring the first of our explanations. In the circumstances we have imagined, then, it seems more likely, that you, not your roommate, are to blame for the missing keys!

Searching for rival, more plausible explanations before going on to test a novel one may bear some unexpected fruit: Our search may turn up a simple and obvious explanation for our puzzle. Several years ago, a resident of Seattle commented in a letter to the editor of the city's major daily newspaper that something was causing tiny scratches and pockmarks in the windshield of his car. Subsequently a lot of others wrote to the paper confirming that this phenomenon was widespread. Articles and letters appeared that attempted to explain this puzzle. People speculated about everything from acid rain to industrial pollutants to mysterious new chemicals used to deice roads in winter. In fact, the correct explanation was considerably simpler: The initial letter encouraged people to look *at* their windshield, not *through* it, and when they did so for the first time they noticed marks and scratches that had accumulated over the years.

An additional advantage to the search for rival, plausible explanations becomes apparent when we consider what happens if our quick check for rival explanations turns up nothing. If we cannot explain away the phenomenon in question, we have some initial evidence that we are on the right track with our proposed explanation. This brings us to the central topic of this chapter.

■
_____

HOW TO TEST AN EXPLANATION

In Chapter 1, we spoke of explanatory stories rather than of explanations. Our point was to emphasize the tentativeness with which novel explanations are issued. Suppose then that we have a novel explanation, call it E, for some puzzling state of affairs. We know of no plausible rival explanation and are confident that we have accurately described the puzzling phenomenon. How do we determine whether E is the correct explanation for our puzzle?

To test E, we need to design an experiment that will provide some sort of independent evidence either for or against E. The fact that E, if correct, would explain our puzzle is not evidence that E is correct. What we need is a set of experimental conditions under which we can predict that something very specific will occur if E is the correct explanation but not if it is incorrect. Recall for a moment our earlier discussion of the puzzle involving your missing car keys. One explanation we proposed was that your roommate had inadvertently taken your keys. The fact that your keys are missing is not evidence that this is right. Remember the other explanations we considered for the missing keys. As all our proposed explanations stand in the same relation to the puzzling facts, the puzzling facts cannot be construed to provide evidence for the correctness of any of the explanations.

To actually provide evidence, we could begin by assuming your roommate has taken your keys. Based on this assumption, we could contact your roommate and ask about the keys with a very specific prediction in mind: that your roommate will acknowledge having taken your keys by mistake. If your roommate were to indeed acknowledge it, we would have independent evidence for the explanation at issue. Moreover, if your roommate were to deny having taken the keys, we would have evidence the explanation must be mistaken.

This is roughly the strategy followed in designing tests for explanations in science. First, we attempt to arrive at a set of experimental conditions under which we can predict the following:

1. Something quite specific will happen if the explanation is correct.

2. This thing will not happen if the explanation is wrong.

In other words, we want to try to arrive at a set of experimental conditions under which the predicted result will occur if and only if the explanation at issue is correct.

Our prediction, of course, must be something other than the puzzling facts we are trying to explain. If in addition conditions 1 and 2 are satisfied in the design of an experiment, the results will reveal either that the explanation at issue is correct or mistaken. To see this, consider the conclusion we are entitled to draw once our experiment has been conducted. First, imagine that we fail to get the predicted result. Condition 1 tells us that if the proposed explanation were right, we ought to get our result. So if we do not, we have evidence our explanation must be wrong. Next, imagine we do get the predicted result. Condition 2 tells us that if the proposed explanation were wrong we should expect to get something other than the predicted result. Thus if we do get the predicted result we can conclude that the explanation must be right.

One crucial concern in designing a test that meets both conditions 1 and 2 is to impose a measure of control, much as we did in designing a test for causal links in Chapter 2. We discovered there that without information provided by a control group we cannot determine whether an effect is due to a suspected cause. Suppose, for example, we have determined that a group of subjects exposed to a suspected cause develops the effect in question. Lacking the kind of benchmark a control group provides, we cannot say the effect is due to the suspected cause; the effect may be due to some other factor. But if we find the effect represented at a significantly different level in a control group, we have evidence that effect and suspected cause are linked.

Similarly, condition 2 is designed to impose a level of control in tests for explanations; it requires that we arrive at a prediction that will not occur unless the explanation is correct. It is not enough that the predicted result occurs if the explanation is right, as is required by condition 1, because the result may be independent of the explanation. That is to say, it may occur if the explanation is right but also if it is wrong.

Tests of explanations can and often do involve experimental and control groups. This is often the best way to ensure that condition 2 is satisfied. In such an experiment, the predicted result is a difference between what occurs in the experimental and control groups that we would not expect to find if the explanation were wrong.

However, the use of control groups is not the only way to meet condition 2. Consider, for example, the experiment described in the following news story:

Satellite Supports 'Big Bang' Theory

Phoenix—A NASA satellite has provided powerful evidence supporting the "big bang" theory, which holds that the universe began over 15 billion years ago with the most colossal explosion ever.

John C. Mather, an astronomer with the space agency, said Thursday that precise measurements by the Cosmic Background Explorer [COBE] satellite of the remnant energy from the big bang has given readings that are exactly as the theory predicted.

The theory, first aired in the 1920s, posits that all matter in the universe was once compressed into an exceedingly small and super-heated center that exploded, sending energy and particles outward uniformly in all directions. At the moment of the explosion, temperatures would have been trillions and trillions of degrees and have been cooling ever since.

If the theory is correct, astronomers expected an even distribution of temperatures just fractionally above absolute zero to still exist in the universe as an afterglow from the explosion.

Mather said that a COBE instrument called the Far Infrared Absolute Spectrophotometer has now taken hundreds of millions of measurements across the full sky and has determined that the primordial temperatures are uniformly distributed. He said the uniform temperature left from the big bang is 2.726 degrees above absolute zero—or about minus 456.9 degrees F.[5]

This story reports on the results of an experiment done to provide new evidence for an explanation most astronomers and cosmologists accept: the big bang theory. (Even the most well-entrenched explanations can benefit from further confirmation, particularly if they involve elements such as the big bang theory that cannot be directly observed.) The theory predicts a uniform temperature throughout the universe and consists of millions of measurements taken across the full sky.

Now, this experiment clearly satisfies condition 1. If the big bang theory is right, there should be a uniform afterglow. But does it meet condition 2? In other words, is the prediction likely to be true whether or not the big bang theory is correct? The story goes on to say:

> Craig Hogan, a University of Washington astronomer, said the new research "is verifying the textbooks" by providing powerful evidence for the theory. Hogan said that the COBE results exactly match the theoretical curve of temperature energy decay that would be expected in the big bang theory.

This new passage suggests that the specificity, both of the prediction and the explanation, ensures compliance with condition 2. The match between prediction and experimental results is so nearly perfect that it seems highly unlikely unless the theory is right.

Ideally, we have said, a good test of an explanation should satisfy conditions 1 and 2. Unfortunately, we do not live in an ideal world; rarely if ever do actual experiments provide the kind of decisive evidence our experimental strategy promises. In the real world where scientific experiments are actually carried out, it would be nearly impossible, for example, to arrive at a prediction that simply couldn't occur if the explanation at issue were wrong. In anything other than unrealistic and utterly ideal conditions, happenings can and do upset our expectations. Even in the case of the missing car keys, things could undermine our test results. Perhaps your roommate is unwilling to admit taking your keys or is unaware of having done so. Either would suggest our proposed test may not provide totally conclusive evidence for or against our explanation.

Our experimental strategy is valuable not because it sets a realistic standard but because it provides us with an idealized standard against which we can assess the design of actual experiments. The closer an actual experiment comes to meeting our two requirements, given the constraints of the real world, the better its design.

■

A CASE STUDY

Let us apply what we have said so far about the design of a good experiment to an actual case. One of the more interesting episodes in the history of science involves the theory of spontaneous generation. As recently as the late 1800s many people believed that living organisms could be generated from nonliving material. One physician in the 17th century, for example, claimed that mice arose from a dirty shirt and a few grains of wheat placed in a dark corner. Similarly, it was thought that maggots—tiny white wormlike creatures, the larval stage of common house-flies—were generated spontaneously out of decaying food. In 1688, Italian physician Francesco Redi published a work challenging the doctrine that decaying meat will eventually turn into flies. The following passage is from Redi's *Experiments in the Generation of Insects*:

> I began to believe that all worms found in meat were derived directly from the droppings of flies, and not from the putrefaction of meat, and I was still more confirmed in this belief by having observed that, before the meat grew wormy, flies had hovered over it, of the same kind as those that later bred in it. Belief would be vain without the confirmation of experiment, hence in the middle of July I put a snake, some fish, some eels from the Arno and a slice of milk-fed veal in four large wide-mouthed flasks; having well closed and sealed them, I then filled the same number of flasks in the same way, only leaving these open. It was not long before the meat and fish, in these second vessels, became wormy and flies were seen entering and leaving at will; but in the closed flasks I did not see a worm though many days had passed since the dead flesh had been put in them.[6]

This passage gives us Redi's explanation for the development of maggots, a description of the experiment he carried out to test his explanation, and his test results.

To determine whether Redi's experiment meets our criteria for a good test, it will be useful to have at our disposal a concise description of the explanation, experimental conditions, and prediction involved in Redi's experiment. In the passage we just read, Redi provides us with his results, rather than his predicted results, but we can easily extrapolate back to the prediction Redi had in mind when designing his experiment:

> *Explanation:* Worms are derived directly from the droppings of flies (E1).

> *Experimental conditions:* Two sets of jars are filled with meat or fish. One set is sealed and the other left open so flies can enter (EC1).

> *Prediction:* Worms (maggots) will appear only in the second set of jars (P1).

Earlier we pointed out that a good test of an explanation will be one in which, under the right experimental conditions, we can predict the following:

1. Something quite specific will happen if the explanation is correct.

2. That specific thing will not happen if the explanation is wrong.

So we must ask two questions about Redi's experiment.

1. If E1 is correct, is it highly likely that P1 will occur under EC1?

2. If E1 is wrong, is it highly unlikely that P1 will occur under EC1?

The answer to the first question is relatively easy. If the worms are derived from the droppings of flies, it would seem highly likely that only the meat in the open containers would develop worms. But assume for the moment that Redi's predicted results are not obtained. Assume that worms appeared in the sealed containers as well or that no worms appeared in the exposed meat. It is at least possible that E1 could be true even if P1 failed to occur. It may be, for example, that the seals were not perfect, in which case fly droppings might be able to contaminate the sealed jars; or it might be that flies did not lay eggs in the unsealed containers. What this means is that a failure to obtain P1 can be taken to show that E1 is mistaken only if we make certain assumptions, namely that neither of the possibilities we have just mentioned are likely to be the case. Because precautions could be taken to ensure that the seals were perfect and because it seems highly unlikely that flies would somehow avoid the open containers, the failure of P1 to obtain would seem to provide quite decisive evidence against E1.

The two possibilities we have just considered are examples of *auxiliary assumptions*. In just about any test of an explanation, there are bound to be assumptions that must hold if a successful prediction is to count decisively for the explanation or even if failure is to count decisively against it. Auxiliary assumptions can be thought of as adding an "unless" clause to our two conditions. A good test will allow us to predict the following:

1. Something quite specific will happen if the explanation is correct unless some auxiliary assumption turns out to be false.

2. The specific thing will not happen if the explanation is wrong unless some (though perhaps different) auxiliary assumption turns out to be false.

As you can see, it is quite important to think about crucial auxiliary assumptions both in designing and evaluating experiments. But this poses something of a problem: We can hardly hope to specify all of the things that could go wrong in designing and carrying out an experiment. For example, in any experiment involving apparatus, we must assume the apparatus is operating properly and that it gives accurate measurements. We must also assume the people operating the apparatus know what they are doing and are recording their results accurately. I suppose we must even make assumptions about their character—that they would, for example, not intentionally engage in fraud. Where do we start and where do we stop in thinking about auxiliary assumptions?

The trick is to limit ourselves to thinking about specific things that both stand some realistic chance of occurring and that would thereby compromise the experiment. In Chapter 1 we discussed the work of Ignaz Semmelweis on childbed fever. Recall that Semmelweis had physicians wash their hands in chlorinated lime water as a means of cleansing themselves of cadaveric matter. A crucial auxiliary assumption made by Semmelweis was that the lime water would eliminate all traces of cadaveric matter. If this assumption were false, the test would have failed even if Semmelweis's explanation were correct.

Specificity is an important requirement of auxiliary assumptions. We cannot explain away a failed prediction on the ground that something unanticipated or not fully understood happened. The point of thinking about possible auxiliary assumptions is to anticipate specific things that could have an impact on the experiment. To vaguely allude to the possibility of such things is not to give an auxiliary assumption. One difficulty we face in evaluating experiments in areas with which we have only a passing familiarity is that we may just not know enough to anticipate crucial assumptions. Nonetheless, it is always worthwhile to spend a little time thinking about possible auxiliary assumptions when working with an experiment.

Now, think once again about the prediction in our case study: Redi's claim that worms will appear in only one set of containers. Would a failed prediction rule out Redi's explanation? No, not if either of the auxiliary assumptions discussed earlier turned out to be mistaken. What if both held—the jar seals were perfect and fly droppings were detected in the unsealed containers? Could we be certain Redi was wrong? Once again no, for it is always possible that other things we are unaware of could undermine this conclusion. But other possibilities seem remote; certainly we have not managed to articulate any. Thus, on balance, a failed prediction under these circumstances would constitute quite strong evidence against E1.

Now consider the second question. If E1 is wrong, is it highly unlikely that P1 will occur under EC1? If worms are *not* derived from the droppings of flies, does it seem highly unlikely that worms would develop only in the unsealed containers? At first blush, it may seem the answer is straightforward. If the worms are produced by some process internal to the meat and fish, not by fly droppings, it would seem highly improbable that worms would develop in just those containers left exposed to the air. Thus if the predicted result occurs it seems we have strong evidence that E1 must be correct. It would just be too much of a coincidence if the predicted results occurred even though E1 is incorrect.

However, things are not always as straightforward as they seem. Many scientists of Redi's time believed in the doctrine of spontaneous generation and looked upon his results with some suspicion. They speculated that there might be some "active principle" in the air necessary for spontaneous generation. By depriving the meat and fish in the sealed containers of a sufficient flow of fresh air, they reasoned, Redi may have inadvertently prevented the spontaneous generation of worms. So although Redi's experimental results seemed to confirm E1, they appear consistent with the doctrine of spontaneous generation.

In light of this line of speculation, the answer to 2' must be carefully qualified. If E1 is wrong, it is highly unlikely that P1 will occur under EC1, but only if we can make certain additional auxiliary assumptions. The major assumption, of course, is that there is no "active principle" in the air necessary for the spontaneous generation of worms in meat. But there is a large and more nebulous assumption we must also make: that spontaneous generation does not involve any other process that Redi may have tampered with or overlooked in setting up his experiment. On balance, then, the occurrence of P1 constitutes evidence for E1 only if we can be reasonably sure our auxiliary assumptions hold.

Our examination of the work of Francesco Redi, given our two requirements for optimal experimental design, suggests that Redi's results were not entirely decisive. Based on his experiment we can be certain neither of the truth of his explanation nor of the falsehood of the doctrine of spontaneous generation. This much we can say, however: Redi designed and carried out an experiment that provided strong initial evidence of something amiss in the doctrine of spontaneous generation. He certainly made clear the kind of assumption that would have to hold if the doctrine of spontaneous generation were to survive mounting experimental evidence that it is wrong: something like an "active principle" in the air would need to be worked out and tested if the doctrine of spontaneous generation were to remain viable. In fact Redi did find a simple and quite decisive way of testing for this active principle, but this is another story—one that, by the way, you will be asked to think about in just a bit. But our story has a happy ending. Building on the work of Redi and others, later researchers were able to dispatch the doctrine of spontaneous generation. Their work made use of a new scientific instrument, the microscope, to make careful observations of bacteria and other microorganisms not visible to Redi.

Several points about the nature of scientific experimentation are nicely illustrated by the example we just considered. First, the results of a single experiment rarely provide decisive confirmation of an explanation. Rather, they often make a tentative finding and point in the direction of needed further experimentation, much as Redi's experiment pointed to the need for a further experiment involving free-flowing air.

Second, even if the results of an experiment are negative we need not conclude that the explanation is wrong, for we have at our disposal a number of alternatives. Imagine, for example, that we have carried out an experiment but failed to get the result we predicted. We could, of course, conclude that our proposed explanation is wrong. But we need not do this yet. We might decide rather that we made an auxiliary assumption we were not entitled to make, or that the experimental conditions were somehow compromised. In our example, failure to properly seal the first set of containers would constitute a defect in the experimental conditions; the assumption that freely circulating air is not required for spontaneous generation might constitute an auxiliary assumption that bears closer examination. By this maneuver we may be able to "save" an explanation that appears under experimental scrutiny to be wrong. However, if there are no questionable auxiliary assumptions and no reason to believe the experiment flawed, such holding maneuvers will do little good. The point is that in designing an experiment it is important to be aware both of potentially questionable auxiliary assumptions associated with the explanation and of possible weakness in experimental design.

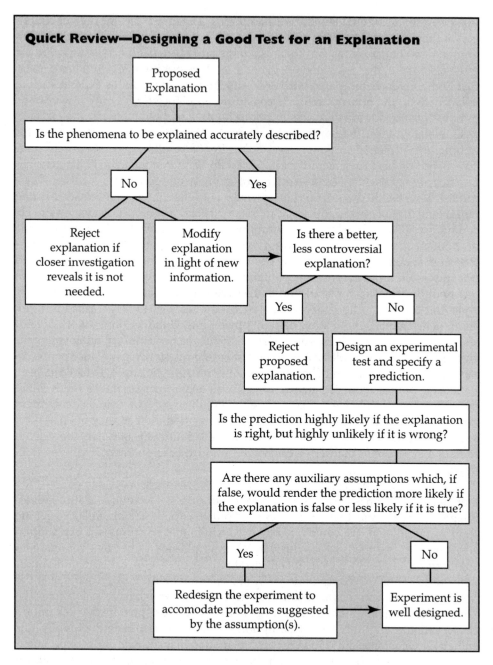

Quick Review—Designing a Good Test for an Explanation

Proposed Explanation

Is the phenomena to be explained accurately described?

No | Yes

Reject explanation if closer investigation reveals it is not needed.

Modify explanation in light of new information.

Is there a better, less controversial explanation?

Yes | No

Reject proposed explanation.

Design an experimental test and specify a prediction.

Is the prediction highly likely if the explanation is right, but highly unlikely if it is wrong?

Are there any auxiliary assumptions which, if false, would render the prediction more likely if the explanation is false or less likely if it is true?

Yes | No

Redesign the experiment to accomodate problems suggested by the assumption(s).

Experiment is well designed.

Finally, a good experiment need not be one that confirms the explanation at issue. Had Redi's experimental results been contrary to his prediction and had all attempts to "save" the explanation failed, his experiment would nonetheless have been a good one. The point of an experiment is to provide decisive results one way or the other given the constraints of the real world. A good experiment, then, will tell us when an explanation is right or at least on the right track but it will also tell us when a proposed explanation is in all likelihood wrong.

■_____

HOW NOT TO TEST
AN EXPLANATION:
A CASE STUDY

If you have a cat or dog you may have noticed that on occasion your pet seems to react to things before they happen and sometimes even to know what you are thinking. Whenever I'm angry, for example, my cat seems to sense it and makes a point of avoiding me. When I'm in a good mood, she invariably follows me around, hoping for attention and snacks. Is it possible that extrasensory perception (ESP) is the explanation for this remarkable behavior? Consider the following test, proposed in a book entitled *Test Your ESP*:

> At mealtime you might put out two feedpans instead of one for your dog or cat. The feedpans should be located so that they are equally convenient to the animal. They should be placed six to eight inches apart. Both should contain the same amount of food and avoid using a feedpan the animal is familiar with. Pick the dish you wish the animal to eat from and concentrate on it. In this test, the animal has a 50% chance of choosing correctly half the time. You may want to keep a record of his responses over several weeks to determine how well your pet has done.[7]

The explanation at issue here is that animals are receptive to human thoughts via ESP and the prediction is that under proper experimental conditions pets will pick the dish we are thinking of more than 50% of the time (not a 50% chance "half the time" as the author of the passage claims).

Assume now that cats and dogs do indeed have ESP. Does it follow that our experimental subject should pick the bowl we are thinking of more than 50% of the time? In other words, is it clear we have isolated a result that ought to occur provided the explanation at issue is correct? Yes, but only if one highly questionable auxiliary assumption is granted. Suppose you were to say to your pet, in an entirely monotonous tone of voice, "Eat out of the red dish, the dish on the left, Fido." I doubt Fido would grasp the meaning of the words you have uttered. Domestic animals tend to react to a complex of behavioral cues, some given by vocal inflection, but not to the meaning of words uttered in their presence. Thus if saying aloud "Eat out of the red dish" will not do the trick, it is doubtful that thinking the same thing silently will work. Nor will it do to "picture" in your "mind's eye" the red bowl. I doubt Fido would react in the appropriate way to an actual picture of the bowl, so it seems highly unlikely Fido would react to nothing more than a mental picture of it. Our prediction thus seems to follow from our proposed explanation only if we make a questionable assumption, namely that animals can understand human thoughts and words.

In addition, it does not seem too unlikely that our subject would pick the correct bowl more than 50% of the time even if our proposed explanation were false. A number of things could happen, any of which would account for our subject's success. Here are a few. First, suppose that our subject tends to go to one bowl instead of the other. It is possible that the experimenter, who is both sending the instructions and observing the outcome, will inadvertently think of the dish the pet favors. Second, domestic animals are very good at discerning nonverbal cues. It may be that the experimenter is inadvertently looking at or standing in the direction of the dish being thought about and the experimental subject is picking up these cues. Finally, recall our discussion of confirmation bias earlier in this chapter. Something very much like confirmation bias may be at work here. Suppose our experimenter were convinced before doing the experiment that animals have ESP. In recording or evaluating the subject's responses the experimenter might inadvertently leave out responses that would otherwise provide evidence against animal ESP.

As we said earlier, a good test of an explanation will be one in which, under the right experimental conditions, we can predict two things:

1. Something quite specific will happen if our explanation is correct.

2. The specific thing will not happen if our explanation is wrong.

The prediction associated with our ESP experiment satisfies the first condition only if we grant an entirely questionable auxiliary assumption. But the design of the experiment leaves open so many loopholes—so many ways for the predicted result to occur even if the explanation at issue is false—that we must conclude that the second of our two conditions is not met at all. A good test like Redi's will provide evidence one way or the other about the explanation at issue. A poorly designed test, like the pet ESP test, will leave us precisely where we began: with little reason to think one way or the other about the explanation being tested.

■
_____

SUMMARY

We have covered a lot of material in this chapter, so before concluding a brief review is in order. Here is a summary of what is involved in testing an explanation. Prior to undertaking any sort of test of a novel explanation, we must do a bit of preliminary work. First we determine that we have an accurate description of the phenomenon to be explained. Next, we hunt for rival but more plausible explanations. If by either of these moves we cannot explain away the phenomenon, we are ready to design a test for our novel explanation.

Let's quickly review the key ideas involved in constructing a good experiment:

1. Experimental conditions—a description of the experiment we propose to carry out.

2. The prediction—what we expect to happen under our experimental conditions if the explanation at issue is correct.

3. Auxiliary assumptions—any assumptions we must make in conjunction with our experiment that must hold if either a failed or successful prediction is to provide decisive results about the proposed explanation.

In a well-designed experiment, the prediction will be (a) highly probable if the explanation is correct and (b) highly improbable if the explanation is mistaken. Whenever possible we need to make explicit any questionable auxiliary assumptions required if the prediction is to follow from our explanation. Finally, it is always a good idea to reexamine our experimental design in light of any questionable assumptions; it may be possible to modify the experiment so that questionable assumptions are not required.

■

EXERCISES

Exercises 1–20 involve explanations of one sort or another. For each, answer the following questions:

1. *What is being explained?*

2. *What is the explanation?*

3. *What if any recognizable sorts of explanatory claims occur in the explanation? Your choices are causes, causal mechanisms, laws, underlying processes, or function. Some of the exercises may involve more than one sort of explanation.*

(Note: On page 88 a solution is provided for Exercise 1.)

1. The spinal column is composed of bones (vertebrae) that are separated by cartilaginous pads (discs) that act as shock absorbers for the column. Nerves run out through the spinal cord to the periphery through openings in the vertebral bones. These nerves run very close to the discs, which is why protruding discs can cause pain along those nerves. As a result of injury, infection, or genetic predisposition the disc material can change consistency and produce pressure on the nerves that run out of the spinal cord. This pressure produces pain along those nerves.[8]

2. No one will ever build a flying vehicle that is capable of hovering high in the air while supported by nothing but magnetic fields. This applies to inhabit-

ants of other planets as well. UFO enthusiasts often claim that the flying saucers they "observe" are held suspended in the air and obtain their propulsion from a self-generated magnetic field. However, it is not possible for a vehicle to hover, speed up, or change direction solely by means of its own magnetic field. The proof of this lies in the fundamental principle of physics that nothing happens except through interactions between pairs of objects. A space vehicle may generate a powerful magnetic field, but in the absence of another magnetic field to push against, it can neither move nor support itself in midair. The earth possesses a magnetic field, but it is weak—about 1% of that generated by a compass needle. For a UFO to be levitated by reacting against the earth's magnetic field, its own field would have to be so enormously strong that it could be detected by any magnetometer in the world. . . . And, finally, as the magnetic UFO traveled about the earth, it would induce electric currents in every power line within sight, blowing our circut breakers and in general wreaking havoc. It would not go unnoticed.[9]

3. As a boy swimming in the fundamentally rather chilly waters of Massachusetts Bay in summer, I discovered, as others had done before me, that for comfort in swimming, the water near the shore was apt to be warmer when the wind was blowing onshore—toward the shore—than when blowing offshore. By thoroughly unsystematic statistical methods I tested the discovery and found it to be true. But why should it be? I shall try to give the essentials of what I believe to be the correct though obvious explanation without spelling it out in all its logical but boring rigor.

   Warm water tends to rise. The sun warms the surface water more than the depths. For both reasons, surface water tends to be warmer than deeper water. The wind acts more on surface water than it does on the depths, displacing it in the direction of the wind. Accordingly, the onshore wind tends to pile up the warmer water along the shore, while an offshore wind tends to move it away from the shore, where, by the principle that "water seeks its own level," it is continuously replaced by other water that, because it can only come from the depths, must be relatively cold. Therefore, water along the shore tends to be warmer when the wind is blowing onshore than when it is blowing offshore.[10]

4. Most Christians still believe in the Risen Jesus. . . . For example, a Harvard poll taken in 1994 found that 87% of Americans believe that Jesus was raised from the dead. But a survey conducted last month by the Barna Research Group, a conservative Christian organization in Glendale, Calif., finds that 30% of "born again" Christians do not believe that Jesus "came back to physical life after he was crucified." Nor does Berman New Testament scholar Gerd Ludemann, a visiting professor at Vanderbilt Divinity School. To him, the Resurrection is "an empty formula" that must be rejected by anyone holding a "scientific world view." In his latest book *What Really Happened to Jesus: An Historical Approach to the Resurrection* (147 pages, Westminister John Knox

Press), Ludemann argues that Jesus' body "rotted away" in the tomb. The Risen Christ that appeared to the Apostle Peter, according to Ludemann, whose book evoked a roar of protest from German Christians, was a subjective "vision" produced by Peter's overwhelming grief and "guilt" for having denied Jesus when he was arrested. For the Apostle Paul, who had previously persecuted Christians, his vision of the Risen Jesus was the resolution of an unconscious "Christ complex." And what the New Testament describes as Jesus' appearance to "more than 500" followers was a "mass ecstasy."[11]

5. **New Gardenburger Plant Loses Steam**

The new high-efficiency production plant envisioned by Wholesome and HJ Earth Foods Inc. still may become a reality, but the company is reassessing the proper capacity and timing for the plant. Part of the reason for rethinking the production plant is that the Portland-based company's net income dropped 17% in 1995's fourth quarter. Wholesome and Hearty, which makes the Gardenburger and other meatless products, blamed the earnings drop on soft sales coupled with higher legal and marketing expenses.[12]

6. **OSU Researchers Develop Incredible Shrinking Compound**

Heat expands substances, cold contracts them. That's one of the first scientific laws kids learn in school—usually accompanied with an example of heat turning water to steam and cold turning water to ice. Put an asterisk next to the law. Researchers at Oregon State University have developed a compound known to steadily shrink rather than swell when heated over a nearly 2000 degree temperature range. Called zirconium tungstate, the compound could eventually wind up in circuit boards and other electronic, optical, and structural applications where heat plays a role.

Heat in nearly all substances causes atoms to move more rapidly, taking up more space and causing the materials to expand. But the new compound contracts—called "negative thermal expansion"—as it is heated from about minus 450 degrees to nearly 1500 degrees F.

Zirconium tungstate's structure is a combination of zirconium, tungsten, and oxygen atoms—ZrW_2O_8. The vibration of the oxygen atoms that bind the atoms of zirconium and tungsten together is what gives the compound its unique behavior. As the temperature rises, the oxygen atoms vibrate more strongly and pull the other atoms closer.[13]

7. **Q: What makes snow?**

A: Snow begins as rising mist from the ocean or dew from leaves. The molecules of water rise in the warming sunshine, bounding around. They rise as vapor until they are in the high cold air and the vapor molecules begin turning to solid water. One solid water molecule joins with another and then a third one comes along. Soon they form a six-sided figure. The molecules keep their six-sided pattern as they grow into their six-sided flake. Water molecules, made up of an oxygen and two hydrogen atoms, hold on to one another only in a certain way that always forms a hexagon.[14]

8. **Florida Mother Accused of Making Daughter, 8, Ill**
   Fort Lauderdale, Fla.—Jennifer Bush, the Coral Springs, Fla. girl who spent much of her eight years beneath surgeon's knives, tethered to tubes and pumped full of medicine, will remain in state care until a judge decides whether the child's mother intentionally made her ill.
   "We've got probable cause beyond question," Broward County Circuit Judge Arthur Birken said Tuesday as he ordered the state social service agency to keep the child in protective custody. Birken quoted the child's psychologist who said taking Jennifer from her home would be the "safe" decision. Health officials and prosecutors believe her mother, Kathy, has Munchausen-by-proxy syndrome, a psychological condition in which a parent, usually a mother, purposely makes a child ill to get attention.[15]

9. In 1961, President John F. Kennedy, after meeting with his advisors, approved a CIA plan to invade Cuba (with 1400 Cuban exiles) and overthrow the government of Fidel Castro. The invasion, at the Bay of Pigs, was a total disaster. The invaders were killed or captured, the United States was humiliated, and Cuba moved politically closer to the Soviet Union. How did the President and his advisors arrive at such a disastrous decision? Psychologists have long understood that group members who like each other and who share attitudes and interests—like a President and his most trusted advisors—often suffer from group think—the tendency, in close knit groups, for all members to think alike and to suppress dissent and disagreement.[16]

10. Suppose we built a robot to explore the planet Mars. We provide the robot with visual detectors to help it explore the terrain and to steer it away from danger. It is fueled entirely by solar power. Should we program the robot to be equally active at all times?
    No. The robot cannot see at night and might propel itself off a cliff or onto rocks. Moreover, it would be using up energy at a time when it was not receiving any. So we would probably program it to cease its activity at night and to "awaken" at dawn the next morning.
    According to the evolutionary theory of sleep, evolution equipped us with a regular pattern of sleeping and waking for the same reason. The theory does not deny that sleep provides some important restorative functions. It merely says that evolution has programmed us to perform those functions at a time when activity would be inefficient and possibly dangerous. Note, however, that sleep protects us only from the sort of trouble we might walk into, it does not protect us from trouble that comes looking for us! So we sleep well when we are in a familiar, safe place, but we sleep lightly, if at all, when we fear that burglars will break into the room or that bears will nose into the tent.[17]

11. One of the more amazing facts of recent political history is that President Nixon secretly taped the conversations he held with his advisors on how to handle the Watergate affair. And it was information documented on these tapes that finally led to Nixon's resignation. Why would he have recorded these damning conversations? Nixon claimed he decided to tape all goings-on in the Oval Office to provide information for future historians.

12. PCs are selling like hotcakes right now. Why? Well, there has been so much competition among computer manufacturers that prices have dropped to an all-time low. You can buy a PC today for half of what you would have paid five years ago and get a much more powerful, sophisticated one to boot. It's just the law of supply and demand: The quality of goods demanded in a given time period increases as its price falls.

13. Polar bears evolved their white color as a means of camouflage. You see, polar bears are predators and predators benefit from being concealed from their prey. Polar bears stalk seals resting on the ice. If the seal sees the bear coming from far away it can escape. And since the arctic environment is predominately white, the polar bear's white fur serves as an effective means of camouflage.

14. Scoring is down throughout the National Basketball Association this year and one player, Center Chris Dudley, thinks he knows the reason. "I think the defense is better," Dudley said. "I also think one thing that has been overlooked is the fact this summer was the biggest summer ever for player movement. You've got a lot of new teams with a lot of new faces. Usually, it takes the offense a little while to catch up in that case."[18]

15. I had my roof replaced and my house painted because I intend to put it on the market in the spring and these improvements will add to its value.

16. A little-known fact is that the Spanish influenza of 1918 killed millions and millions of people in less than a year. Nothing else—no infection, no war, no famine—has ever killed so many in such a short period. Why then did people pay so little attention to the epidemic in 1918 and why have they so thoroughly forgotten it since?

   The very nature of the disease and its epidemiological characteristics encouraged forgetfulness in the societies it affected. The disease moved so fast, arrived, flourished, and was gone before it had any but ephemeral effects on the economy and before many people had the time to fully realize just how great was the danger. The enormous disparity between the flu's morbidity and mortality rates tended to calm potential victims. Which is more frightening, rabies, which strikes very few and, without proper treatment, kills them all, or Spanish influenza, which infects the majority and kills only two or three %? For most people, the answer is rabies, without question.[19]

17. A softly glowing ball of light appears in the air nearby, hovers for a few seconds, passes through an object and then vanishes. It's a phenomenon known as ball lightning, which appears during thunderstorms as a luminous sphere about the size of an orange or grapefruit.

    Observers have reported seeing ball lightning for centuries, only to be greeted with skepticism. Now, two physicists from the Universidad Complutense in Madrid, Spain, describe a possible explanation for ball lightning; something called an "electromagnetic knot," in which lines of an electric or magnetic field join to form a closed knot.

    The researchers say the lines of force are powerful enough to trap a lump of the glowing hot, electrically charged gas larger than can be created in a thunderstorm. Temperatures in the ball may reach more than 50,000 degrees Fahrenheit. But the energy soon dissipates, the knot untangles, and the luminous ball disappears into thin air.

18. Societies without exception exert strong cultural sanctions against incest. Sociobiologist E. O. Wilson posits the existence of what he terms "a far deeper, less rational form of enforcement," which he regards as genetic.

    Because of recessive genes, children of incest carry a higher risk than others of mental retardation, physical deformity, and early death; they are therefore less likely to mate and reproduce than are children of parents who avoid incest. Hence individuals with a genetic inclination against incest contribute more genes to succeeding generations.

19. Considering how much civic pride in America is invested in having a skyscraper taller than anyone else's, people may wonder why a skyscraper may not grow as high as a city's citizens may wish. The answer is obvious when pointed out; unless the upper stories are to remain uninhabited, the proportion of floor space allocated to elevators in the lower stories soon becomes grossly uneconomic—a truth of which we are vividly reminded by those tall buildings on which the elevators crawl up the outside.[20]

20. The availability of jobs in just about every profession is bound to ebb and flow. Today there is a demand for teachers and a glut of nurses. A decade ago, the situation was just the reverse: too many unemployed teachers and not enough nurses. This is all due to the fact that people tend to opt for training in areas where jobs are currently available. As more and more people in that area come onto the job market, the number of candidates for jobs exceeds the number of available jobs. Hence less and less people opt to train in that area with the net result that within a few years there are not enough trained professionals to fill the available jobs. When this happens, more people elect to train in the underemployed area and the cycle repeats itself.

Exercises 21–30 contain both sets of puzzling facts and proposed explanations of the facts. Work carefully through each exercise, doing all of the following:

1. *State the facts to be explained and the proposed explanation.*

2. *Answer the following preliminary questions:*

   a. *Are the facts of the case as they appear to be?*

   b. *Can you think of any reason to think the facts misrepresent what is going on?*

   c. *If so, how can we determine what the facts are?*

   d. *Do any rival but more plausible explanations come to mind? What are they?*

3. *If you are satisfied that we have a real puzzle, design an experiment in which the explanation given in the exercise can be tested. In other words, imagine a set of experimental conditions and an accompanying prediction that is both of the following:*

   a. *Highly probable provided the explanation is correct.*

   b. *Highly improbable provided the explanation is mistaken.*

4. *Think carefully about any auxiliary assumptions that may be required by your experiment yet that may themselves be questionable. Are there things you may be assuming to be true that, if false, would undermine your results?*

5. *Modify the design of your experiment in light of any questionable assumptions you have unearthed.*

6. *If you have identified a plausible rival explanation, design a test that meets the conditions set forth in step 3.*

(Note: A solution is provided for Exercise 21 on page 88. Look it over carefully to get a sense of how to solve the other problems.)

21. Recently I have noticed something peculiar and really quite irritating about my doctor. If my appointment is for early in the day, I usually see my doctor within a few minutes of the appointed time. But when my appointment is later in the day, I've spent as much as an extra hour sitting in the waiting room or waiting in the examination room. I think I know what the problem is. Whenever I come in for an appointment, my doctor insists on catching up on the details of my life; he asks about my work, my family, how much I'm exercising, even if I've seen any interesting movies or read any good books lately. It seems clear to me that my doctor spends way too much time chat-

ting with his clients about things not related to the problem they are there to see him about. As a result, he falls further and further behind as the day goes on.

22. As you know, Francesco Redi claimed that the worms found on rotting fish and meat are the result of eggs dropped by flies. As you also know, Redi's claim was not universally accepted. Redi's critics hypothesized that there might be something in freely circulating air, something we might call an "active principle," that must be present if spontaneous generation is to occur. (Hint: The explanation to be tested here is not Redi's but rather the one involving the "active principle.")

23. Earlier I mentioned that I have had problems reading small print as the day wears on. I also mentioned that I suspect this is due to eye fatigue. It now occurs to me that this may not be the explanation. It may just be that the intensity and amount of light decreases in the late afternoon and evening. Could this be the source of my problem?

24. From time to time, one hears stories of strange, almost unbelievable animal behavior. Pets, for example, seem to sense when their master is about to return. Dogs and cats have been known to move their young to a safe place just before an earthquake. There are many documented cases in which animals have reacted strangely to their impending death or that of their masters. These incidents involve knowledge that came to the animals in some apparently paranormal way. There is no apparent explanation for them except ESP.

25. A fact of life in large organizations—whether in the private or the public sector—is that an enormous number of people are doing jobs for which they are not qualified. This is because of what is often called the Peter Principle: People tend to rise to the level of their incompetence. In a large organization, if you are good at what you do you will be promoted. And if you are competent at your new job you will be promoted once again. The process of advancement stops only when a person rises to a position where they are not fully competent. Lacking competence, they will do a poor job and thus not be promoted further. So a person's final position in a large organization will be one they are not qualified to fill.

26. Many of you have probably played with a Ouija board. On a rectangular board approximately 2 feet by 3 feet are printed all of the letters of the alphabet, the numbers 1–10, and the words "yes" and "no." A small, plastic, three-legged stool called a planchette is placed on the Ouija board. Two people sitting on opposite sides of the board rest the tips of their fingers gently on opposite ends of the planchette. Somebody then asks the spirit of the Ouija board a question and what follows is startling. The planchette slowly begins to move and often spells out an answer to the question! What is more, the

answer is frequently something that neither of the participants have any way of knowing. The spirit may even predict something that is yet to happen. As anybody who has played with the Ouija board will attest to, one has the distinct feeling that the planchette is actually pulling the hands of the participants about the board; the participants do not feel as though they are pushing the planchette. Well, this is just wrong. In fact the participants are moving the planchette. The eerie feeling of being dragged about the board results from the fact that each participant is exerting only half as much effort as it would take a single person to move the planchette. The resulting impression—that something else is doing the work—is thus understandable. But this "something else" is not the spirit of the Ouija. It is the person on the other end of the planchette.

27. A recent telephone survey of 113,000 Americans about religious affiliation came up with some rather interesting facts. Perhaps the most interesting was that while nationwide 7.5% of respondents say they belong to no church, 15% of the sampled residents of Oregon, Washington, and California claim no religious affiliation. It seems clear that all the "new age" mumbo jumbo that goes on out West is turning people away from God.

28. Recently, a good friend quit her job. This is surprising because her income was in the six-figure range as a partner at a large law firm. And guess what she is doing now? She sold her home and bought a tiny, primitive cabin in the woods where she lives alone and claims to be studying to become a Buddhist monk! She says she has enough money put away to live for a year or so and afterward doesn't know what she is going to do. This amazes me because she has always been such a responsible person. You know what I think? She's undergoing a good old-fashioned midlife crisis.

29. The following is from a newspaper editorial entitled "Books Now Being Sold by the Pound":

   According to assurances by the publishers, Norman Mailer's new novel, *Harlot's Ghost,* is tough to put down. It is also, at 1328 pages, no snap to pick up. And when you put it down, you might want to make sure there are no small children underneath.

   Mailer's new book is the most dramatic example of ink inflation, the new tendency for books to come in at a size and heft that used to be reserved for stereo speakers. Currently, a good middle-weight novel can run 800 pages.

   The strange thing about this epidemic of book bloat is that books are getting longer just as, everyone agrees, the time spent reading is getting shorter. At two minutes a page, *Harlot's Ghost* would fill up about 50 hours, which is just about the total annual reading time of entire American age groups.

   People have several ideas on why books are getting so much longer than the average attention span. Basically, of course, the reason is technology. Right now, most books are written on word processors, meaning that by pushing a single button the writer can turn a research note into a page. It also means that writing on at length is essentially painless, except for the person who tries to read it.

Back when people wrote with quill pens, or even with manual typewriters, writers had to think a little more about whether what they were about to say was worth the effort of writing it. Not surprisingly, the calculation made for shorter books.[21]

30. The following story appeared about an advertisement in a weekly news magazine as well as in the local newspapers. It seems that the Pepsi-Cola Company decided that Coke's three-to-one lead in Dallas, Texas was no longer acceptable, so they commissioned a taste preference study. The participants were chosen from Coke drinkers in the Dallas area and asked to express a preference for a glass of Coke or a glass of Pepsi. The glasses were not labeled "Coke" and "Pepsi" because of the obvious bias that might be associated with a cola's brand name. Rather, in an attempt to administer the two drinks in a blind fashion, the Coke glass was simply marked with a "Q" and the Pepsi glass with an "M." Results indicated that more than half chose Pepsi over Coke. It seems clear that, when the effects of advertising are set aside, cola drinkers prefer the taste of Pepsi to Coke.[22]

A Solution to Exercise 1

1. *What is being explained?* The manner in which a protruding disc can cause nerve pain.

2. *What is the explanation?* Nerves run very close to discs, and when discs are injured or infected they can change consistency and protrude. This in turn causes pressure on the nerves, which results in pain.

3. *What if any recognizable sorts of explanatory claims occur in the explanation?* The passage explains that a disc problem can cause nerve pain. It does so by discussing the intervening causal mechanism: the sequence of events, beginning with damage to a disc and ending in lower back nerve pain. The passage also gives a functional explanation of the vertebral discs: They serve as a kind of shock absorber.

A Solution to Exercise 21

(Note: Don't simply accept this solution. Satisfy yourself that the experiment is a good one! If you spot any problem, try to improve on the experimental design.)

1a. *State the facts to be explained and the proposed explanation.* The fact to be explained is my doctor's failure to stay on schedule. The explanation proposed is that he spends a good deal of the allotted time with his clients discussing extraneous things.

2a. *Are the facts of the case as they appear to be?* This is hard to say, but one thing seems clear here: My belief is that my doctor is routinely late, but most people don't go to the doctor all that often and I am no exception. So it seems likely my belief is based on a small number of observations.

2b. *Can you think of any reason to think that the facts misrepresent what is going on?* Apart from the possibility mentioned in the proposed explanation, it may be that I simply remember those few aggravating instances in which I was kept waiting and that they have occurred late in the day by coincidence.

2c. *If so, how can we determine what the facts are?* We could easily keep a record for a month or so of all appointments and the actual times that clients were seen.

2d. *Do any rival but more plausible explanations come to mind? What are they?* Assuming that it turns out, on the basis of something like the investigation described in 2b, that my doctor does fall further and further behind on a routine basis, several rival explanations come to mind. (I'm sure you can think of others.) One is that emergencies often come up requiring that he take time away from his scheduled patients. Another (actually suggested by a doctor) is that clients frequently schedule appointments to deal with a single ailment but during the examination bring up other problems that require additional time to investigate.

3. *Design an experiment in which the explanation given in the passage can be tested.* The explanation at issue is that my doctor spends too much time talking with his clients about things having no obvious bearing on the problem for which the client is being seen. Keep in mind that we are not trying to establish whether my doctor chats too much with his clients, but whether extraneous chatting is the reason he falls behind schedule. We might test this explanation by obtaining his cooperation and instructing him to consciously refrain from speaking with clients about things not directly related to the problem they are there to see him about. We might then videotape (with client permission, of course) all his appointments for a week. If our explanation is right, we would predict that my doctor will stay on schedule or, at any rate, come closer to staying on schedule.

In this experiment, the prediction seems both highly probable if the explanation is correct and highly improbable if it is wrong. If extraneous chatting with clients is the correct explanation, we would expect time per appointment to decrease. Moreover, if our explanation is wrong it seems highly unlikely that we could reduce time per visit by simply limiting the amount of extraneous chatting.

4. *Think carefully about any auxiliary assumptions that may be required but that may themselves be questionable.* One important but rather nebulous auxiliary assumption comes to mind: Our experiment involves the assumption that the instructions we give the doctor—indeed, the doctor's knowledge that he is taking part in an experiment—will have no effect on the way he works. It seems possible that he will inadvertently work more quickly because he is nervous or aware of being part of the experiment. If either is the case, any improvement noted over the course of the experiment may be due to factors other than that for which we are testing.

5. *Modify the design of your experiment in light of any questionable auxiliary assumptions you have unearthed.* Asking the doctor to work at a normal pace may just make things worse. However, we might take the precaution of taping a week's worth of appointments prior to giving the doctor his instructions. We can then use the first week's tape as a rough benchmark against which to judge whether he is performing at a normal rate during the week of the experiment.

6. *If you have identified a plausible rival explanation, design a test that meets the conditions set forth in step 3.* If our test yielded negative results—if under the conditions we have described my doctor were to continue to fall behind— we might want to consider one of the rival explanations proposed in step 2d. The most likely one lies in the suggestion that clients routinely want to discuss ailments in addition to those they indicate when making their appointments. The details of an effective test for this explanation are not too difficult to work out. Here again, we must be clear on what we are testing. At issue is not whether people complain of additional maladies but whether such complaining is the source of the problem we are investigating. To this end we might design an experiment that involves instructing the doctor to deal only with the problem for which a client is seeing him. Or we might instruct the person who schedules appointments to make sure that clients give a complete inventory of problems prior to their visit. Of course, care must be taken to insure that our prediction meets the conditions in step 3.

Notes

1. In fact, there is now evidence that some crop circles are man-made. Several people claim to have made circles and have demonstrated to the British media how to make them! (*See* Nickell and Fischer, "The Crop Circle Phenomenon," *Skeptical Inquirer*, v. 16, no. 2., 1992.)

2. This example is adapted from John Elster's *Nuts and Bolts for the Social Sciences*, Cambridge: Cambridge University Press, 1989, a very readable account of prominent causal mechanisms used in the social scientific explanation.

3. The studies on which this example is based describe the situation before a vaccine for hepatitis B was developed. It is interesting to note that before the advent of the vaccine, chances of dying from accidental exposure to hepatitis B were almost identical to those today associated with accidental exposure to HIV. Yet the hepatitis B risk receives much less attention than that given today to accidental HIV exposure in the medical community.

4. The use of "razor" here derives from Ockham using his principle to "shave away" certain metaphysical entities that philosophers of the time generally believed in. Ockham used the razor to argue, for example, that abstractions are not "real" beyond the words used to express them. One can, in Ockham's view, account for the significance of such expressions without introducing the notion of corresponding abstract entities.

5. Recer, Paul. "Satellite Supports Big Bang Theory." Associated Press, Jan. 8, 1993.

6. Redi, Francesco. *Experiments in the Generation of Insects* (1688). Translated by Mab Bigelow. Chicago: Open Court Publishing, 1909.

7. Ebon, Martin (ed.). *Test Your ESP.* New York: Signet, 1970, p. 73.

8. Hister, Art. *Dr. Art Hister's Do-It-Yourself Guide to Good Health.* Toronto: Random House, 1990, p. 178.

9. Rothman, Milton A. *A Physicist's Guide to Skepticism.* Buffalo: Prometheus, 1988, pp. 148–149.

10. Homas, George. *The Nature of Social Science.* New York: Harcourt, Brace & World, 1967, p. 21.

11. Woodward, Kenneth L. "Rethinking the Resurrection." *Newsweek,* Apr. 8, 1996, pp. 62–63.

12. From *Oregonian,* Apr. 5, 1996.

13. From *Oregonian,* Apr. 5, 1996.

14. Marvin, Rob. "What in the World." *Oregonian,* Jan. 21, 1993.

15. Leinwand, Donna. Knight-Ridder News Service, in *The Oregonian,* Apr. 17, 1996.

16. Adopted from Wade and Tavris. *Psychology.* 2nd ed. New York: HarperCollins, 1990.

17. Kalat, James W. *Introduction to Psychology.* 2nd ed. Belmont, Calif.: Wadsworth, 1990, p. 103.

18. Quoted in "NBA Teams Merge into the Slow Lane," *The Oregonian,* Nov. 25, 1996.

19. Crosby, Alfred W. *America's Forgotten Pandemic: The Influenza of 1918.* Cambridge University Press, 1989, p. 321.

20. Medawar, P. B. *The Limits of Science.* New York: Harper & Row, 1984, p. 69.

21. Sarasohn, David. Editorial. *Oregonian*, Oct. 3, 1991. ©1991, *Oregonian*.

22. Adapted from a case study in Huck, Schuyler W., and Sandler, Howard M. *Rival Hypotheses.* New York: Harper & Row, 1976.

CHAPTER
FOUR

Extraordinary Claims and Anecdotal Evidence

EXTRAORDINARY CLAIMS

In Chapters 2 and 3 we examined the methods by which causal links and explanations are tested. On occasion, however, the focus of a scientific investigation will be neither. People make extraordinary claims about things they have experienced and things they can do, and these can be tested by methods similar to those discussed in Chapters 2 and 3. Precisely why such claims should be of interest to science is something we will consider in a moment. But first let's try to get a better sense of what the extraordinary involves by looking at a number of extraordinary claims.

Some people claim to be able to see colorful "auras" emanating from the human body and to be able to discern things about one's personality by careful study of these auric emanations. Others claim to have been contacted by extraterrestrials or to have seen alien space craft—unidentified flying objects or UFOs—hovering in the night sky. Astrologers claim to be able to predict things about your future based on the position of the planets at the time of your birth. Similar claims are made by people who read palms, tea leaves, and tarot cards. Many people claim to have psychic ability of one sort or another: to be able to see the future, read the minds of others, or manipulate objects by sheer mind power. Some claim to have seen ghosts, poltergeists, or assorted cryptozoological creatures—everything from bigfoot to the Loch Ness monster. Many claim to have lived past lives or to have left their bodies during near death encounters. Others claim to have communicated with the spirits of long-dead people.

On occasion, scientists make extraordinary claims. In March of 1989 two scientists, Stanley Pons and Martin Fleishmann, announced that they had created nuclear fusion at room temperature in a test tube; what makes this so extraordinary is that nuclear fusion usually takes place only at hundreds of millions of degrees. Some linguists and psychologists claim to have taught chimpanzees and gorillas to "speak" using American Sign Language. Around the turn of the century, a group of reputable French physicists claimed to have observed a new kind of electromagnetic radiation that they called "N-rays." This last example differs from the first two in that within five years of being discovered N-rays were conclusively shown not to exist. By contrast, a few physicists and chemists continue to believe that cold fusion may be possible, though the vast majority disagree; and though experimenters have worked with chimpanzees and gorillas for over thirty years now, their findings remain controversial—some critics contend that the experimental subjects are only mimicking speech behavior, occasionally giving the right signs in response to questions and the like but not really using language, at least in the sense that humans do.

Many extraordinary claims involve healing and medicine. Some dentists claim we are being poisoned by our fillings. Iridologists claim to be able to diagnose illness by examining nothing more than the iris of the human eye. Faith healers claim to heal all sorts of illness and disability by prayer and the laying on of hands. Psychic surgeons claim they can perform operations without the use of anesthetic or surgical instruments. The list of extraordinary things people claim to have seen and done is nearly endless.

All these claims have in common a pair of features. First, they are controversial in that though there is some evidence for the truth of each it is somewhat sketchy. Second, all appear to be at odds with some aspect of our current scientific understanding of the natural world. Suppose, for example, someone claims to be able to levitate. This claim is controversial precisely in that though there is actually some evidence for levitation—photographs and the apparently sincere testimony of people who claim to have levitated—it is limited. Moreover, if levitation is indeed possible then our current understanding of how and where gravity operates will have to be revised.

Or consider the claim made by many psychics to be able to divine the future. The evidence for such an ability is scant: in most cases a few clear and correct predictions accompanied by lots of vague and downright wrong ones. But if some people can actually see what has yet to happen, we must rethink our current view about the nature of causation. Common sense, if nothing else, suggests that if A is the cause of B then A must occur before B. Yet if the future can be seen, effects can be established long before their causes come into existence. Thus if the future can be foretold, something somewhere is wrong with our current view of causation.

Extraordinary claims, then, are both controversial and, if correct, revolutionary in calling for revision of our current understanding of some aspect of the natural world. This latter fact accounts, from a scientific point of view, for much of the interest in extraordinary claims. If we can establish the truth of an extraordinary claim, we have a good indication of where our current scientific understanding of things is either incomplete or wrong. How such claims might be established is our next topic.

■
TESTING EXTRAORDINARY CLAIMS

People known as *water witches* or *dowsers* claim they can detect underground water with a simple forked wooden branch. They loosely grasp one fork in each hand and point the branch straight ahead, parallel to the ground. When they approach a source of water the dowsing rod, as the forked stick is called, will point in the direction of the water much as a compass needle will point toward magnetic north. Many successful dowsers claim to be able to pinpoint sources of water for well drilling or even to have found water where conventional geologists failed.

This meets both of our criteria for the extraordinary claim. First, the actual evidence for dowsing is limited. We must rely on the testimony of dowsers and their clients about past performances. Moreover, if a dowser points to a location and a well is drilled that actually hits water, it does not prove that the dowser actually located it with the dowsing rod. Perhaps it was a coincidence, or maybe there were visual clues to aid the dowser—patches of greenery near the chosen location or something similar. And we have no sense of dowsers' success rates other than what they and their clients report. How often are they mistaken? Second, if dowsing actually works our current understanding of the various forces and interactions operating in the world today will need to be revised and supplemented. Nothing modern science tells us about ourselves and nature suggests that a simple wooden branch in the hands of a person will respond to a source of water.

Our challenge, then, is to devise an experiment that will give us decisive evidence one way or the other about the dowser's claimed ability to find water with nothing more than a wooden branch. In designing an experiment we need to borrow some ideas from our discussion in Chapter 3 of the requirements for a good test of an explanation. We said that a good test involves a predicted result that will occur if the explanation is correct but not if it is mistaken. We also noted that the predicted result must be independent of the evidence the explanation is invoked to explain. In testing for a claimed extraordinary ability, we are not primarily concerned with an explanation for it but rather with whether a person can do the extraordinary thing. Thus in our test we require nothing like an independent prediction. Instead we will try to devise a set of experimental conditions by which we can predict the following:

1. The subject or subjects in question will actually be able to do the extraordinary thing they claim to be able to do.

2. The subject or subjects will not be able to perform if they do not have the ability they claim to have.

Consider now what an experimental test of dowsing must be like to satisfy criteria 1 and 2.

Criterion 1 will be satisfied if we arrive at a set of experimental conditions under which the dowser clearly ought to be able to perform. A good rule of thumb to follow in setting up tests of extraordinary claims so that they satisfy criterion 1 is to consult the experimental subject or subjects prior to designing the experiment. We want to set up conditions under which the experimental subjects will agree in advance that they ought to be able to perform; otherwise failure may be taken to show only that the experiment is hostile to the ability we are attempting to test. But if our subjects concur that the experiment approximates conditions they should be able to perform under, such excuses lose much of their force. If they claim to be able to perform under a given set of conditions, it is hard to take their protests seriously if they complain about the nature of the test after they fail it.

Criterion 2 will be satisfied if we are careful to set up conditions under which there could be no way for the dowser to find water short of detecting it with the dowsing rod. In effect we want to try to rule out the possibility of cheating, coincidence, inadvertent cuing on our part, visual or audio clues as to where the water is, and the like. If we succeed in imposing controls sufficiently tight to rule out these possibilities, success by the dowser can be taken to vindicate his or her claimed extraordinary ability.

Now that we have a sense of what a good experiment ought to involve, let's try our hand at actually designing one. Imagine that we contact one of the country's best known and most successful dowsers and he or she agrees to take part in our experiment. We propose to place before our dowser ten identical large ceramic jars with covers, one containing water and the others empty, arranged in a straight line equidistant from one another. The dowser can approach but not touch any jar. Our subject agrees that he or she should be able to find the single jar with water. If the dowser is successful, a second test will be performed with the jars rearranged (the subject will, of course, leave the room while the jars are being rearranged). As an additional precaution, no one who knows the location of the jar containing water will be allowed in the room while the dowser is being tested.

Does our imagined experiment satisfy criteria 1 and 2? Once again, here they are:

1. The subject or subjects in question will actually be able to do the extraordinary thing they claim to be able to do.

2. The subject or subjects will not be able to perform if they do not have the ability they claim to have.

Criterion 1 is satisfied provided our subject agrees that the conditions we have built into our experiment are conditions under which he or she can detect water. In addition, it does seem highly improbable that a dowser could pick the right jar with no actual ability to dowse, provided all ten jars are identical and provided no one who knows the location of the jar containing water is in a position to give an inadvertent clue to the dowser. Under these conditions, chances are one in ten that the dowser will select the correct jar. However, such odds are not that small. Hence our insistence that the dowser submit to a retest if he or she succeeds in the first trial: the chances of a single dowser selecting the right jar in two successive trials is considerably smaller—one in a hundred. Thus with the retest provision and the precautions we take to eliminate inadvertent cuing, our test satisfies criterion 2; the odds are slim that the dowser would succeed because of lucky guesses.

One feature of our test deserves additional comment. We have been careful to arrive at a prediction that sets a clear line of demarcation between success and failure. If our dowser can find the jar containing water in two successive trials, he or she is successful; anything less constitutes failure. In designing controlled tests it is important to avoid predictions that blur the line between success and failure. Imagine, for example, that we had decided to test our dowser by burying containers of water a few feet below the surface of a vacant lot. The dowser would then be instructed to place markers where he or she believed the containers to be located. Suppose the dowser placed markers within three or four feet of one of the containers. Does this constitute a hit or a miss? Just how far off must a marker be before we consider it a miss? Or suppose markers are placed at ten locations when only five containers were buried and that seven of the markers are within a few feet of one or the other of the containers. How do we evaluate these results? Has our dowser succeeded or failed?

The line between success and failure can be very difficult to draw when a prediction involves some sort of subjective impression on the part of the experimental subject. Imagine, for example, that we were to test a purported telepath—someone who claims to be able to read the thoughts of another. As part of our experiment we instruct the telepath to sketch a simple picture that someone in another room is concentrating on. Suppose the person in the other room is looking at a postcard of a small sailboat moored at a marina and that the telepath produces a simple drawing that includes a vertical straight line and a narrow triangular shape that might correspond to a boat hull or sail. Unfortunately, however, several of the drawing's details conform clearly to nothing we can discern on the postcard. Is the telepath's impression accurate or inaccurate? Presuming we can decide what constitutes a detail or feature of the picture on the card, how many features or details must the telepath get right to be a clear indication of success?

To take another example, imagine that a tarot card reader gives a personality analysis of someone unknown to the reader based on the position and order of the cards. The reading might indicate that the person in question tends to be optimistic despite occasional moments of depression or pessimism, or makes friends easily, or displays clear leadership ability. How do we evaluate such claims? The problem here is not only with the generality of the predictions but with the lack of a clear basis for judging them. We must first arrive at an accurate personality profile of the person; but presuming we could do this, what objective basis do we have for comparing our profile with that of the tarot card reader? No doubt any two sets of subjective impressions about a person's character will contain some words and phrases in common. How much similarity is required to put some stock in the analysis of the tarot card reader?

In designing a test, then, it is crucial that we arrive at a prediction that clearly spells out the difference between success and failure. If in evaluating the results of

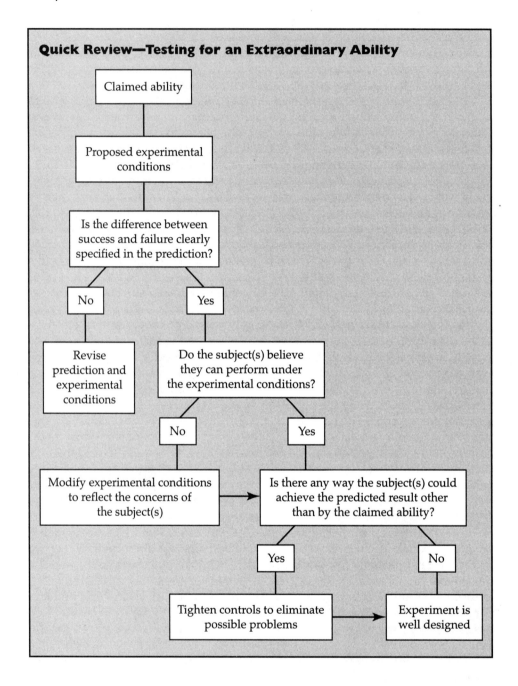

a test we are unable to say precisely whether our subject has succeeded or failed, the test has very little point. It certainly fails to satisfy criterion 2, for we have not specified a result that we could rate as highly unlikely if our subject or subjects did not have the ability in question. Fortunately, however, the prediction in our dowsing test seems to be clear and unequivocal: success and failure are clearly spelled out. So let's return briefly to the dowsing test we have proposed and look at the conclusion we are justified in drawing, depending on the results we get.

If our dowser can consistently find water under these experimental conditions, it is highly unlikely it could be accounted for by anything other than a genuine ability to detect water with a dowsing rod. Of course, if we achieve this result our work will have just begun: we must consider what might explain how the movement of a wooden branch is influenced by the presence of water. Where, that is, are the gaps in our understanding of things that have kept us from understanding this remarkable phenomenon?

But if our dowser consistently fails, chances are high that his or her successes under noncontrolled conditions are no indication of an extraordinary ability. Note here a difficulty that plagues most tests of the extraordinary. Suppose our dowser does indeed fail. Does this show conclusively that dowsing doesn't work? No; we have only shown that our particular dowser does not have this extraordinary ability. Furthermore, if we test (say) ten dowsers and none pass, believers in dowsing might begin to wonder if our test makes some auxiliary assumption that is false. If dowsers in general cannot perform under the conditions of our experiment, so the argument would go, perhaps the experiment is flawed in some way neither we nor the dowsers understand. Perhaps, for example, there is an undetected source of ground water underneath the location of our experiment that interferes with a dowser's ability to function.

To make matters worse, even if we could satisfy ourselves that our experiment is not defective and that we are making no false auxiliary assumptions, we would only be in a position to conclude that none of the dowsers we tested are the genuine article. After all, instances of dowsing have been reported for hundreds of years; the earliest record of a successful dowsing dates to 1586 in Spain. Moreover, over the years thousands and thousands of people have attested to the success of dowsers. What, then, are we to make of negative experimental results given the vast body of historical and contemporary evidence that there is something to dowsing? This brings us to our next topic: anecdotal evidence.

■
_____

ANECDOTAL EVIDENCE FOR THE EXTRAORDINARY

The strongest evidence for an extraordinary claim is that provided by careful controlled testing. But it is not the only kind. Anecdotal evidence—historical reports of extraordinary happenings and reports by people who claim to have witnessed or to have done something extraordinary—at least suggest that extraordinary things do happen. But how do we evaluate such evidence, particularly where it constitutes the sum total of evidence for something extraordinary? Presuming we are open-minded and willing to think critically, what should our attitude be toward extraordinary claims backed largely by anecdotal evidence? Skeptical disbelief? Tentative belief, at least in those cases where the anecdotal evidence is considerable? A kind of scientific agnosticism? An agnostic is a person who claims it is impossible to know whether there is a God or not. We might appropriate this term for our purposes by slightly modifying its standard meaning: a person is an agnostic with respect to a particular claim if he or she believes that the evidence for the claim warrants neither belief nor disbelief. An agnostic, in this sense, maintains that one ought to remain intellectually open to the possibilities suggested by extraordinary claims.

No doubt agnosticism appears the fairest, most objective, and most critically responsible of our three possible responses. Yet frequently it is not. Often scientific agnosticism about anecdotal evidence for the extraordinary amounts to nothing more than a failure to think critically about it. Even where the anecdotal evidence is considerable, skeptical disbelief is warranted more often than not; ironically, the kind of open-mindedness valued by the agnostic often requires disbelief, not agnosticism. To get at the reasons for this, we must explore a bit further the notions of skeptical disbelief and agnosticism. Consider, to begin, the following case.

A famous psychic contends he can bend keys telekinetically—that is, by simply willing them to bend. Hundreds of people claim to have witnessed our psychic perform this extraordinary feat. Typically, he holds an ordinary house or car key in one hand, concentrates his thoughts on it, and before the eyes of witnesses it actually seems to bend! Unfortunately, our psychic refuses to be tested under controlled conditions on the grounds that he finds it impossible to perform in the presence of experimenters who are understandably skeptical. Some things, claims our psychic, are not meant to be tested.

As with most extraordinary claims, however, there is some evidence that this one may not be true. First, our psychic apparently cannot perform under tightly controlled conditions. Why not? Consider the fact that an equally famous magician can do everything our psychic can do, but by out-and-out trickery—nothing psychic is involved at all. It is well known that people can easily be deceived by a skilled magician; we've all seen them make people float in thin air and produce all manner of objects out of nothing. Surely a skilled magician could trick us into believing we have seen a key bend. Of course, under tightly controlled conditions a magician might find it considerably more difficult to accomplish such deceptions.

So what are we to make of our psychic and his extraordinary claim? Is he genuine or a fraud? Based on the evidence we have examined so far, it may seem that this question is impossible to answer and that an open-minded person should withhold judgment pending further evidence. Agnosticism might well seem the proper attitude. But there is a kind of evidence we have not yet considered, a kind that stands in the background of nearly every extraordinary claim.

As we pointed out earlier, extraordinary claims are generally at odds with our current understanding of some aspect of the natural world. A principle that seems well established in nature is that one event cannot influence another without some intervening mechanism or medium. The flow of blood in the human body resists the pull of gravity in part because of the pumping action of the heart. Magnets influence the movement of ferromagnetic particles via an intervening medium, their surrounding magnetic fields. There are in fact no known instances of what is sometimes called "action at a distance"—actions or events causally related to antecedent but remote actions or events wherein there is no intervening medium or mechanism. A variant of this principle seems to hold for human action as well. If I want to bring about a change in the world external to my mind, I must do more than think about it. In general it is well established that a person's mind cannot effect a change in the physical world without the intervention of some physical energy or force. If, say, I want to move an object from one spot to another, simply willing the object to move is insufficient to accomplish my purpose. I must figure out some way— some sequence of actions—that can lead to the goal I will myself to accomplish.

Now, it may turn out that the "no action at a distance" principle is false, that we will eventually discover some phenomenon that involves action at a distance. Imagine, then, that someone claims to be able to do something or to have witnessed something that could only be achieved by action at a distance. Clearly we should require extraordinarily rigorous evidence in its favor before accepting such a claim, for the enormous body of scientific investigation accumulated over centuries is, indirectly at any rate, evidence against it.

What does all this suggest about the extraordinary claims made by our psychic? The slogan "extraordinary events require extraordinary evidence" sums it up nicely. If telekinesis exists—if it is indeed possible to cause remote physical events to happen by force of will—then either action at a distance is possible or there is some subtle medium or mechanism at work that has so far eluded our detection. Because so much is at stake, we are entirely justified in demanding extraordinarily decisive evidence for our psychic's claim to influence objects telekinetically. In the absence of such evidence—evidence of the sort provided by carefully controlled testing, not by anecdotal testimony or even by the apparently sincere avowals of our psychic—we have good reason to doubt his extraordinary ability. If he can do what he claims, we must take seriously the notion that forces or processes are at work in nature that have so far escaped our detection; we must begin thinking about revisions to our current understanding of things.

We began this section with an important question. Given that we are open-minded and willing to think critically, what should our attitude be toward anecdotal evidence for the extraordinary? Tentative belief where the evidence is considerable? Agnosticism? Skeptical disbelief? Where evidence for the extraordinary is entirely anecdotal, our attitude should be one of skeptical disbelief tempered with a willingness to revise our position only in light of well-established experimental evidence. This is because a great deal is likely to be at stake: if the extraordinary can be established, we must set about revising or perhaps even overturning some part of what we currently believe about the nature of things. And since we are likely to have a considerable body of evidence supporting the beliefs in question, we have good reason to retain our skepticism about things extraordinary. This is not to say that extraordinary claims cannot be established, but to suggest that we should remain skeptical until presented with evidence for the extraordinary of sufficient strength and quality to warrant a careful rethinking of the evidence for those beliefs we are being asked to set aside.

The rationale behind this kind of enlightened skepticism is eloquently summed up by Richard Dawkins, professor of zoology at Oxford University:

> Some things that have never been reliably seen are, nevertheless, believable insofar as they do not call in question everything else that we know. I have seen no good evidence for the theory that plesiosaurs live today in Loch Ness, but my world view would not be shattered if one were found. I should just be surprised (and delighted), because no plesiosaur fossils are known for the last 60 million years and that seems a long time for a small relic population to survive. But no great scientific principles are at stake. It is simply a matter of fact. On the other hand, science has amassed a good understanding of how the universe ticks, an understanding that works well for an enormous range of phenomena, and certain allegations would be incompatible, or at least very hard to reconcile, with this understanding. For example, this is true of the allegation, sometimes made on spurious biblical grounds, that the universe was created only about 6,000 years ago. This theory is not just unauthenticated. It is incompatible, not only with orthodox biology and geology, but with the physical theory of radioactivity and with cosmology (heavenly bodies more than 6,000 light years away shouldn't be visible if nothing older than 6,000 years exists; the Milky Way shouldn't be detectable, nor should any of the 100,000 million other galaxies whose existence modern cosmology acknowledges).
>
> There have been times in the history of science when the whole of orthodox science has been rightly thrown over because of a single awkward fact. It would be arrogant to assert that such overthrows will never happen again. But we naturally, and rightly, demand a higher standard of authentication before accepting a fact that would turn a major and successful scientific edifice upside down, than before accepting a fact which, even if surprising, is readily accommodated by existing science. For a plesiosaur in Loch Ness, I would accept the evidence of my own eyes. If I saw a man levitating himself, before rejecting the whole of physics I would suspect that I was the victim of a hallucination or a conjuring trick. There is a continuum, from theories that probably are not true but easily could be, to theories that could only be true at the cost of overthrowing large edifices of successful orthodox science.[1]

The kind of enlightened skepticism exemplified in this passage is likely to be misunderstood. In response to a demand for rigorous evidence, believers in the extraordinary would probably offer something like the following:

> Well, what do you expect from a mainstream scientist? Such scientists are conservative in the worst sense of the word. When presented with new ideas that challenge their pet theories, they just reject the new ideas out of hand rather than even consider the possibility that their accepted theories may be wrong. Were scientists to acknowledge the extraordinary, they would have to admit they

don't know everything and that there may be things science just cannot explain. So the mainstream scientific community has a vested interest in denying the existence of things extraordinary.

Setting aside for the time being the question of whether there are things that science cannot explain, there is something profoundly wrong in this rejoinder. The idea that science is somehow uncomfortable with or embarrassed by the extraordinary is quite the reverse of the actual case. A great number of major advances in the history of science have their roots in attempts at understanding something extraordinary. After all, such things serve to suggest something amiss in the current scientific picture of how the world works. Indeed, science will continue to develop only so long as there remain phenomena that challenge received explanations. Thus, far from finding the extraordinary embarrassing, science has a vested interest in discovering and establishing instances of extraordinary phenomena. An extraordinary claim is of great scientific interest precisely because it does not fit into our current understanding of things and consequently points us in the direction where research needs to be undertaken. So, the initial reaction of the competent scientist when faced with a report of the extraordinary ought to be the kind of enlightened skepticism we have been discussing. The scientist's first task is to try to show that the purportedly extraordinary event has a more or less conventional explanation. Only when this attempt fails can we be confident that the event points toward an area that requires further investigation.

■
_____

DESCRIPTION AND EXPLANATION

Reports of the extraordinary frequently blur the distinction between description and proposed explanation. It may seem that when people report extraordinary events they are simply describing what occurred—no more, no less. But in fact considerably more is likely to be contained in such reports. Imagine, for example, that someone were to report waking in the middle of the night to discover what appeared to be his long-departed grandmother standing at the foot of the bed. He might subsequently claim:

1. I saw the ghost of my dead grandmother.

But what, precisely, is factual in statement 1? What can we be confident actually happened? That the person had an extraordinary experience is clear. Beyond that it is hard to say. Consider two rival accounts of what may have happened:

2. He had a vivid lifelike dream in which his grandmother appeared.

3. Somebody played an elaborate and vicious prank on him in the middle of the night.

All three statements implicitly contain explanations of the event, but each presupposes a very different truth: (1) that what he saw was actually a ghost, (2) that what he "saw" was part of a dream, and (3) that what he saw was real but was a hoax, not a ghost.

Similarly, many anecdotal reports of the extraordinary contain much more than a simple, objective description of the experience. Such reports often blend fact with untested explanation and are what we might call *explanation laden*. For example, "The flying saucer hovered over the horizon and then accelerated away at a fantastic rate" tells us a couple of things about the person who makes the statement. First, the person had an undeniably extraordinary experience; second, the person believes the proper explanation for the experience is the actual existence of an intelligently controlled spacecraft.

In evaluating such a report, we must do our best to separate the descriptive wheat from the explanatory chaff. If we are able to subtract the explanation-laden portions of a report of the extraordinary, we may be able to arrive at a clear sense of what actually was experienced and thus what needs to be explained. For example, suppose we could establish that the person making the flying saucer report actually saw a bright light near the horizon, looked away to call to a friend, looked back again, and saw only a dim, twinkling light at some distance from the original light. Having gotten clear on this much, we would at least be in a position to think about rival explanations more plausible than the one implicit in the initial description of the event.

I once spoke with a person who claimed to have lived in a haunted house. He recalled that every few nights he would hear a knocking at the front door, but there was never anyone there when he opened it. We agreed that a more accurate description of the experience would contain only the salient facts: on several occasions he heard a series of sounds very much like knocking at a door that seemed to come from the area of the house near the front door. He also added that he was never near the door when he heard the noise. Once we focused on this new, more objective description, several plausible explanations immediately came to mind: a tree or bush knocking against the house or some other activity outside or even inside that sounds from a distance like knocking. Now, we may never discover what really happened on those nights when he heard a "knocking" at the door. At the very least, however, we know which parts of the story are fact and which are speculation. And this is the real value of carefully distinguishing between the descriptive and explanatory elements of an extraordinary claim.

EXERCISES

Exercises 1–10 involve extraordinary claims. Design a good test for each. Try to devise a set of experimental conditions under which

> **a.** *The subject or subjects in question will actually be able to do the extraordinary thing they claim to be able to do.*
>
> **b.** *The subject or subjects will not be able to perform if they do not have the ability they claim to have.*
>
> **c.** *The difference between successful and failed performance is clearly measurable.*

In designing your test, think about any auxiliary assumptions the test requires that may be questionable. Are you assuming something to be true that if false might enable your experimental subjects to explain away a failure to perform under the conditions of the test? If you uncover any such assumptions, try to modify your design so that it avoids them. (Note: A solution to Exercise 1 is provided on page 111.)

1. The ability to influence physical objects or events by thought alone is called telekinesis or psychokinesis. One extraordinary claim of people who say they have telekinetic power is an ability to influence the outcome of apparently random events. So, for example, by concentrating on a particular number a person trained in telekinetic manipulation might influence the throw of a pair of dice or the spin of a roulette wheel.

2. Graphologists claim to be able to discern a great deal about a person's character and personality simply by analyzing the person's handwriting. So, for example, if you don't care enough to dot your I's it shows that you tend to ignore details, and an illegible signature indicates a desire to escape notice. Similarly, claim many graphologists, people who print rather than write may be trying to conceal their personality from others.

3. Reflexology is the technique of applying pressure with the thumbs and fingers to specific areas of the feet as a means of alleviating various ailments. Reflexologists contend that the body and all its organs and glands are "mapped" on the foot. For example, the big toe is said to represent the head, the little toe the eyes and ears, and the inner portion along the side of each foot the spine. Some reflexologists claim to be able to diagnose ailments by looking for painful spots on the foot. Throat and tonsil problems, for example, frequently result in pain on the bottom of the big toe whereas pain on the bottom of the other toes often indicates sinus problems.

4. Do you believe in reincarnation—in the notion that we have lived previous lives? Many people claim to recall details of past lives under hypnosis, and in many cases it would seem they have no way of knowing these details without having actually experienced them. The most famous case of reincarnation is that of Bridey Murphy. In 1952, Virginia Tighe was hypnotized and, in that state, reported details of a previous life in Cork, Ireland, as Bridey Murphy. She spoke in a distinct Irish accent that she did not normally have and described her life in Cork in great detail. Many other people have reported similar experiences under hypnosis.

5. For years, mediums have claimed to be able to contact the spirits of the dead. Typically a medium will seat a number of people around a table in a dark room and instruct them to hold the hands of the people next to them, close their eyes, and concentrate. The medium then goes into some sort of trance and, if everything is right, the spirit of a dead friend or relative of one of the participants will speak though the medium and sometimes even answer questions asked of it.

6. Many people who claim to have the gift of psychic power say they are able to see auras—fields of light that surround human beings and possibly other living things. Presumably these auras are internally generated fields of psychic force. Moreover, these individuals claim that one's personality can be identified by the color and form of one's aura and that the colors of an aura will change with a person's mood. (Note: there are two extraordinary abilities involved here: the ability to detect an aura and the ability to give personality analyses based on the colors in it.)

7. Biorhythms supposedly consist of three cycles: physical, emotional, and intellectual. The cycles are 23, 28, and 33 days long, respectively, and all begin at the moment of birth. During positive phases (the first half of each cycle) energies are supposed to be high, and during negative phases energy is low. Critical days occur when one of the rhythms is changing from positive to negative or vice versa. Those days, say biorhythmists, contain our weakest and most vulnerable moments because the rhythms that guide our lives are unstable. The very worst are triple-critical days, when all three rhythms are changing from positive to negative or vice versa. In the first 58 years and 68 days of life there are 4006 single-critical days, 312 double-critical days, and 8 triple-critical days. Taken together, critical days make up about 20% of all the days of a life. Needless to say, a person should expect to perform poorly in aspects of life corresponding to the particular rhythm in flux on a critical day. On triple-critical days, biorhythmists will tell you, you should just stay in bed.

8. Some individuals claim they can leave their body at will and travel through space using only their "astral" or "spiritual" body. This ability is often called

astral projection. Some claim they can travel almost instantaneously to the far corners of the world; others claim even to visit other planets and planetary systems. All are able to report in detail on what they have experienced during their astral excursions. Some parapsychologists contend that astral projection is the first solid scientific evidence for the existence of the soul.

9. Everyone knows that Egyptian mummies have remained remarkably well preserved for thousands of years. The reason, claim some people, is that the mummies were entombed in pyramid-shaped structures, and in some way not yet understood, that shape focuses a mysterious form of energy on objects housed within it. Advocates of pyramid power claim, for example, that organic matter of just about any sort can be preserved if housed under something with the shape of a pyramid.

10. As long ago as the mid-1960s, researchers began reporting success in teaching primates to communicate using American Sign Language. Washoe, a chimpanzee, and Koko, a gorilla, were apparently able to learn and use many signs to form complete sentences and to reply to questions asked them by researchers who themselves communicated with Koko and Washoe in sign language.

Exercises 11–15 involve actual anecdotal reports of the extraordinary. Assess each by answering the following questions:

    a. What if any well-established principles does the report challenge?

    b. Is the report explanation laden? If so, what is the implicit explanation?

    c. Is there a plausible nonextraordinary explanation for the reported event?

    d. What should our attitude be toward the report: skepticism, agnosticism, or tentative belief? Why?

11. Barney and Betty Hill were returning from a vacation in Canada when they reportedly saw a UFO. Barney then inexplicably turned their car left onto a side road, and that was all the Hills remembered until two hours later, when they found themselves 35 miles further down the road with no idea how they got there. The Hills began to have bad dreams and finally went to see a psychiatrist, Benjamin Simon, who used hypnotic regression to bring them back to the incident. Under hypnosis, the Hills said that extraterrestrials had impelled them to leave the car and walk to the spacecraft, where they were separated and given examinations. Betty said alien creatures stuck a needle in her navel and took skin and nail samples. Barney claimed they took a sample of his sperm.

12. A species of monkey that lives on several islands off the coast of Japan is often fed by humans. In 1953, a remarkable thing was reported. One member

of the troop of monkeys on one island learned to wash the sand off sweet potatoes she was given by dunking them in the ocean. Other members of the troop quickly picked up the habit, and then the remarkable happened: once enough monkeys had learned to wash potatoes, suddenly all monkeys even on other islands hundreds of miles away knew how to do it. It would seem that when the idea reached a "critical mass"—when it was known by a sufficient number of monkeys—it mysteriously spread to the species as a whole.

13. On a few rare occasions, living human beings appear to have mysteriously ignited and been largely consumed by fire. Though there are no well-documented, witnessed instances of spontaneous human combustion, in a number of cases the remains of a person strongly suggest it happened. Typically the body will be almost entirely destroyed by fire that begins in the torso, often leaving a limb or two intact; this contrasts markedly with most burn injuries, where the limbs are affected first. In spontaneous human combustion, the body is reduced to greasy ashes—even the bones. There is often no apparent source of flame and little damage to the victim's surroundings.

14. In 1975, George and Kathy Lutz purchased a house in Amityville, New York. The year before, six members of the previous owner's family were murdered in the house by another family member. Within hours of moving in, claim the Lutzes, horrible and astonishing things began to happen. Large statues moved about the house with no human assistance. Kathy Lutz levitated in her sleep. Green slime oozed from the walls. Mysterious voices were heard, sometimes saying, "Get out, get out." A large door was mysteriously ripped off its hinges. Hundreds of flies appeared seemingly from nowhere. After only 28 days, the Lutzes left their new home for good.

15. In March 1984, reporters were invited to the home of John and Joan Resch to witness evidence of a poltergeist—a noisy and rambunctious spirit. The reporters found broken glass, dented and overturned furniture, smashed picture frames, and a household in general disarray. The focus of all this activity seemed to be the Resch's 14-year-old adopted child, Tina. The destructive activity, claimed the Resches, always occurred in close proximity to Tina. Objects would mysteriously fly through the air, furniture would overturn, and pictures hanging on the wall would fall to the floor, all with no apparent physical cause. Because Tina was a hyperactive and emotionally disturbed child who had been taken out of school, some parapsychologists hypothesized that the strange happenings were the result of telekinesis, not poltergeist activity.

16. Each of the anecdotal reports in Exercises 11–15 contains an assertion about the existence of something extraordinary:

a. Alien abductions

b. The instantaneous generation of ideas throughout a species

c. Spontaneous human combustion

d. Ghosts and hauntings

e. Poltergeists

f. Telekinesis

Although all these are quite unlikely, some seem more unlikely than others. Given what we have said about claims that challenge our current understanding of things, rate the relative likelihood of a through f, from most to least likely. Give your reasons for your ratings. Here you will want to consider the possibility of prosaic explanations for the reported events as well as the relative level of evidence for the principles each appears to call into question.

17. The following story appeared in 1992 in major newspapers across the country. Comment on the design of the experiment described, its results, the attitude of the experimenters toward their experimental subject, and the extraordinary ability they tested. What is your conclusion? Is the last sentence of the story accurate?

One reason my family likes going to Chinese restaurants is for the fortune cookies. The fortunes get passed around, laughed at and commented on. Sometimes they are remarkably accurate, or at least that's our impression. I bet there are a lot of people who remember a fortune that was "right on." How is it they fit our personal situation so often when who gets which cookie is purely random?

Well, of course, the fortunes are written in such a general style that they can fit most anyone, but there is a more subtle effect: positive memory. With unusual events, we will always remember the remarkable coincidences and forget the times when nothing of note happened. This accounts for much of the "strange behavior" reported at full moon, for much of the "success" of astrologers and for the persistence of belief in palm readers. Because people remember the "hits" and forget all the "misses," such pseudo-science practices tend to get more credence than they deserve.

This effect is particularly difficult for scientists to deal with. When we debunk astrology, there will always be someone in the room that tells of all the times the astrologer has "read" them exactly right. No matter how logically we argue that astrology can't and doesn't work, it's hard to explain away positive, personal testimony. What we need are controlled experiments that can prove or disprove astrologers' claims.

Such experiments are hard to arrange because astrologers always say that the stars "impel," they don't "compel." In other words, astrologers don't generally make statements that are right or wrong, they make statements that are more or less likely to be true. It's hard to "make or break" a likelihood.

Luckily, we found an astrologer who was willing to make a testable claim. He said that given four horoscopes, only one of which was produced from a person's correct birth date and time, he would be able to identify the correct chart solely from that person's physical appearance. A colleague, Philip Ianna, and I decided to take him up on his claim and run an experiment to see how well he could do.

We arranged to collect the birth dates and times from a number of students in a large astronomy class. In order to insure that there was no error or collusion, we only used students who could provide a copy of their birth certificate. In addition, the astrologer claimed his method would only work on white Anglo Saxons. Thus, no African Americans, Hispanics, American Indians, or Jews were chosen. While he never made it clear why his method would fail in these cases, we nonetheless selected from the student volunteers only those who fit his criteria.

We were convinced from the beginning that if there was to be any useful conclusion drawn from our experiment, we had to carry it out under conditions that would be fully agreeable to the astrologer. Further, we made the experiment as "double blind" as we could. My colleague made all of the contacts with the astrologer, showed him the horoscopes, and was present for the meetings between the astrologer and the students. I, on the other hand, made all of the contacts with the students. I was the one who selected the student population to be used. I was the one who arranged for the correct horoscope, and I was the only one who had the key to the correct birth dates.

After culling the students to fit the astrologer's criteria and adjusting for those who could not miss classes to meet the astrologer, we had exactly 28 students participating, split about evenly between men and women. We called in the students and had them meet, one by one, with the astrologer. He sat at a desk with the four horoscopes for that student in front of him. After looking at the students for a minute or two and hearing a few words from the student, he selected one of the horoscopes as the correct one. The letter (A through D) corresponding to that horoscope was placed on the list next to the number that represented the student.

This process was repeated for all 28 students, and then the astrologer's list was compared with the correct list that had been kept locked in my office. He got seven right—exactly the number that would have been predicted from pure chance. The astrologer could not explain why he had failed to do what he claimed to be able to do. Our conclusion was that his claims were bunk.

Based on what we can find out, the claims of astrology are all bunk but it is not often that science gets a chance to test them in so definite a way.[2]

▪

A Solution to Exercise I

The first thing we need to do in designing our experiment is to set up conditions under which subjects cannot perform unless they have telekinetic ability. The problem with things like dice and roulette wheels is that we will get some result whether or not telekinesis is operating. Suppose a subject were to try to make a die show the same number on every throw. Whether or not the subject has telekinetic ability, the die is bound to show the selected number about one time out of six because there are six sides on a die. No matter how well our subject does, we will be unable to rule out coincidence. What if the die comes up with the given number just a little more or less than one time in six? It would be hard to evaluate. Just how much more than a sixth of the time provides evidence of telekinesis? Much better would be an experimental result that occurs *only* if our subject or subjects have telekinetic ability.

With this in mind, we might begin by contacting people who claim to have telekinetic power, convincing them to take part in our experiment and finding out about the conditions under which they agree they can and cannot perform. To simplify things, let's assume we have selected one likely candidate to be tested. Assume also that the subject is not too specific about how and where telekinesis works but believes he or she should be able to perform under these conditions:

A small, spherical foam ball is sealed in a glass container on a well-anchored, immovable surface. The experimental subject sits with hands in lap a few feet from the surface and is instructed to move the ball by telekinesis.

It seems highly unlikely that the ball will move if the subject does not have telekinetic ability, so success would provide strong evidence for telekinesis. If the subject succeeds and we have any doubts about the outcome, we can easily repeat the whole procedure.

But what if the subject fails? Our experiment involves several auxiliary assumptions, any one of which, if false, could explain the failure: (1) telekinesis does not work with foam, (2) telekinesis cannot move an object this massive, (3) telekinetic force cannot penetrate glass, or (4) telekinetic force falls off over distance and the distance between subject and object was too great. By slightly manipulating the experimental conditions we could probably eliminate the need for any of these assumptions. We might, for example, try objects made of different materials and masses, move the subject closer, or leave the objects to be manipulated out in the open. (In this last case, we must take precautions to ensure that the subject cannot blow on the object if it is very light.)

Notes

1. Dawkins, Richard. *The Blind Watchmaker.* London: W. W. Norton, 1986, pp. 292–293. Reprinted by permission of the publisher.

2. Tolbert, Charles R. "Scientist, Astrologer in Horoscope Showdown." *Oregonian,* July 2, 1992. Reprinted by permission of the author.

CHAPTER

FIVE

Fallacies in the Name of Science

WHAT IS A FALLACY?

The faith of most people in the credibility of science is nearly unshakable. When we read in the newspaper or see on television that there is "new scientific evidence" for X or that "scientists have discovered" Y, our tendency is to assume that the evidence for X or Y is impeccable. Certainly the material we have covered in the previous chapters suggests that careful scientific investigation is the most powerful tool we have for getting at the truth, but the methods used by the scientist to investigate the natural world can be abused.

In this chapter we examine a number of fallacies committed in attempting to employ the methods introduced in the last three chapters. In logic, a fallacy is a mistake in reasoning. Thus, if I conclude that because (1) Morris is a mammal and (2) dolphins are also mammals then (3) Morris is a dolphin, I am guilty of a fallacy—a mistake in reasoning—because 3 does not follow from 1 and 2 even if both are true. Similarly, a fallacy in applying the methods of science occurs when one draws a conclusion one is not logically entitled to draw given the evidence available.

Keep in mind here the difference between fallacious scientific reasoning on the one hand and a mistaken scientific belief on the other. Many ideas in the history of science have turned out to be mistaken, but not because they were products of fallacious reasoning. Prior to the mid-18th century, for example, scientists believed in the existence of *phlogiston*, sometimes called the "fiery substance."[1] Phlogiston was thought responsible for a number of observable reactions in matter. Among other things, it was believed to be the stuff released rapidly into the atmosphere during combustion and slowly as metals decay. But there is no such thing as phlogiston; the scientists of the time were mistaken. Still, the theory of phlogiston reactions was well supported by a large body of experimental evidence—indeed, the best evidence available at the time—and it had served well; for example, the formulas for producing metals from ores were derived from phlogiston theory. However, subsequent experimentation revealed a better explanation for reactions accounted for by pholgiston theory, one involving a new chemical element later identified as oxygen. The point is that the work that established phlogiston theory and the work that ultimately overturned it both involved correct applications of the experimental methods we have been discussing.

By contrast, a fallacy occurs when the methods of science are illicitly applied. Proper applications of scientific method may, as in the case of phlogiston theory, lead to inaccurate results. But they are inaccurate results arrived at by honest investigation. Fallacious applications of the methods of science lead only to a false impression that something has been established with great care and rigor. Indeed, many of the fallacies we shall consider involve ways of lending the appearance of scientific evidence when there is little or none.

One well-known fallacy in informal logic is called *argumentum ad hominem*— attacking the person rather than his or her argument. If, for example, I argue that every student ought to know something about science and so ought to read this book, you might reply that I receive a royalty from the sale of copies of the book. If the point of your reply is to mount an objection to my argument, you are guilty of an ad hominem fallacy. Even though what you say is true, the point you make is not relevant to the argument I have given. By pointing out that I stand to profit if students buy this book, you attack my motives for arguing as I have but you have not shown that my argument is defective.

At the risk of committing an ad hominem fallacy, let me propose the following. Most though certainly not all of the fallacies we will discuss are committed typically by people on the fringes of science, not by mainstream scientists.[2] By "people on the fringes of science," I mean those who engage in fallacious scientific reasoning for either of two reasons: because they have little knowledge of what rigorous scientific inquiry involves but nonetheless believe they are capable of undertaking such inquiry, or because they do know a great deal about science but are trying to create the impression that there is a real measure of scientific evidence for something when there is actually very little. Errors of the sort we will discuss can be committed inadvertently, but sometimes they are intentional. Later in this chapter we will have more to say about the distinction between mainstream science and fringe science or pseudoscience, but for now let's begin looking at various types of scientific fallacy.

Our discussion of scientific fallacies centers around three important questions that need to be asked in any scientific investigation:

1. What precisely are the facts of the case?

2. If an explanation is required, have we carefully considered all plausible rival explanations prior to proposing a novel explanation?

3. If a novel explanation is required, can we devise an effective test for its correctness?

Associated with each of these questions are a number of fallacies. The first set involves mistakes in making initial observations of apparently puzzling phenomena. The second set involves failure to consider rival hypotheses. The final set involves mistakes in the testing of explanations and of claims of extraordinary abilities.

Fallacies Involving Initial Observations

Anecdotal evidence. In Chapter 3 we discussed the dangers of basing generalizations on anecdotal evidence; such generalizations are all too frequently misleading because they are founded on memorable but atypical cases. For example, I've noticed that when I need to do last-minute preparation for an upcoming lecture, a student invariably knocks on my office door. What is it with students? Do they just have an instinctive sense for the wrong time to come to see me? I'll leave it to you to comment on the fallacy in my observations.

Omitting facts. One way to make something appear mysterious is to ignore certain facts in describing the phenomenon, facts suggesting that it may not be all that mysterious. In Chapter 3, we mentioned the apparently puzzling phenomenon of crop circles—large symmetrical geometric figures, circular and otherwise, that have mysteriously appeared in wheat and corn fields in southern England. What we failed to mention is that near almost every crop circle, in some cases even running through the circles, are tram lines, the indentations made by tractors as they travel through the fields. One of the most puzzling things about crop circles is that they are said to exhibit no sign of human intrusion, no footprints or bent plants leading to them, and thus it seems unlikely that they are hoaxes. But though there are no signs of intrusion, it is conceivable that a person could simply walk in the tram lines to the point where the circle was to be constructed without leaving any signs. Accounts of the crop circles, then, retain much of their mystery only when the facts about tram lines are conveniently omitted.

Another example involves the strange happenings said to occur in the Bermuda triangle, an expanse of several thousand square miles off the coast of southern Florida. Hundreds of boats and planes have disappeared in the area over the years. Books about this phenomenon typically describe in great detail cases in which it is clearly documented that a boat or plane known to be traveling in the vicinity of the Bermuda triangle has disappeared, never to be heard from again. Yet two interesting facts are conspicuously missing in most of these reports. First, in many instances wreckage is subsequently found, suggesting an accident rather than a mystery. Second, in just about any expanse of ocean this size near a highly populated area such as the east coast of Florida there will be a number of disappearances due to accidents, storms, inexperienced sailors and pilots, and the like. Only when these facts are omitted do the disappearances in the Bermuda triangle take on an air of great mystery.[3]

Distorting the facts. Another way to create a sense of mystery is to subtly change the content of a factual description. For example, much research has been done in recent years on near-death experiences. Some researchers claim that people who have been near death, typically during a medical emergency, but were revived have reported a remarkable experience. Here is an account from one of the best-known books on the subject, *Life After Life* by Raymond Moody:

> A man . . . begins to hear an uncomfortable noise, a loud ringing or buzzing, and at the same time feels himself moving very rapidly through a long dark tunnel. After this he suddenly finds himself outside of his own physical body, but still in the immediate physical environment, and he sees his body from a distance, as though he is a spectator . . . After a while, he collects himself and becomes more accustomed to his odd condition. . . [and] soon other things begin to happen. He glimpses the spirits of relatives and friends who have already died, and a loving warm spirit of a kind he has never encountered before—a being of light—appears before him. . . . At some point he finds himself approaching some sort of barrier or border, apparently representing the limit between earthly life and the next life. Yet he finds that he must go back to earth, that the time for death has not yet come.[4]

Now, if this precise experience were reported by many people, we would have quite a remarkable thing on our hands. In fact, the description in this passage is based on the reports of hundreds of people. But no two reports are precisely the same; this description combines elements from many varied experiences. Moreover, no single element in it occurs in all reports and no single subject has given precisely this description. Though Moody quite openly admits all of this, many people who argue that near-death experiences provide evidence of life after death accept this artificial account as an accurate description of the strange experiences people report when near death. People are liable to report any number of things, their reports are frequently at odds with one another, and many people when near death report no such experience: all these suggest that there may be a more mundane explanation for the phenomenon. At any rate, the appearance of a great mystery here is exacerbated by the subtle fabrication of an experience that, strictly speaking, no one has ever had.

Quick Review: Observational Fallacies

- **Anecdotal evidence:** Basing a general claim on a few atypical cases

- **Omitting facts:** Creating an air of mystery by ignoring information that may suggest an explanation

- **Distorting facts:** Blending fact and fiction to create the illusion of a genuine mystery

Fallacies Involving Rival Explanations

Fallacious argument by elimination. Suppose we know that either A, B, or C must happen and subsequently discover that B or C will not happen. Logically we can conclude that A will happen. This pattern of reasoning is sometimes called *argument by elimination*, for it involves establishing one alternative, A, by eliminating the possibility of all others. A fallacious argument by elimination occurs when possibilities other than A, B, and C are ignored in the process of arguing for one of the explicit alternatives. Imagine that I want to establish a particular explanation. I list possible rival explanations and then proceed to show that none of them can be correct. Have I established my favored explanation? For two reasons, the answer is no. First, there may be other explanations I have failed to consider. Second, even if I succeed in ruling out all the rival candidates we can think of, the failure of these rival explanations only entitles us to conclude that the phenomenon in question needs explaining, not that my favored explanation is correct.

A common strategy in extrasensory perception (ESP) research is to claim that an explanation involving some sort of extrasensory mechanism can be established by showing that experimental subjects can achieve results in an ESP experiment that would be highly unlikely by chance or luck alone. So, for example, a study might claim that a particular experimental subject has the gift of mental telepathy (the ability to read the mind of another) because she is able to guess the playing card an experimenter is thinking about more frequently than chance would suggest. Implicit in this claim is a fallacious argument by elimination. That the subject is telepathic follows only if we assume that there are only two possibilities—that the subject did it either by telepathy or by sheer luck—and can effectively rule out luck under tightly controlled experimental conditions. But the assumption is flawed. First, there may be other possible explanations: Maybe an invisible imp peeks at the cards and whispers the right answer in the subject's ear. As wild as this seems, it would appear to be as well supported by the experimental outcome as the telepathy hypothesis.[5] Second, even in the absence of rival explanations the outcome of this experiment does not confirm the claim that the subject has telepathy. The only conclusion we are warranted in drawing based on the results of this experiment is that something quite interesting is going on, something we do not fully understand. We are conspicuously not entitled to conclude that we have evidence for any particular explanation.

Fallacious inference to a causal link. In Chapter 2, we considered the kind of evidence required to establish a causal link. People all too often draw conclusions about causal links based on sketchy evidence. In most cases, the inference of a causal link seems plausible only because rival explanations are overlooked or ignored. Conclusions about a causal link between A and B are often drawn on the basis of a number of specific kinds of evidence, none of which taken alone is sufficient to support a claim of causal connectedness. The most prominent of these are the following:

1. A simple correlation between A and B

2. A concomitant variation between A and B

3. The fact that A precedes B

Now consider examples of each of these and two plausible rival explanations for each that they fail to take into consideration.

A simple correlation between A and B. In Chapter 2 we noted that the simplest sort of correlation is a claim about the levels of a characteristic in two groups of which only one has a second characteristic. Thus A is correlated with B if more A's than non-A's have B. This does not necessarily mean that A and B are causally linked, but people frequently make the illicit inference that they are.

Imagine that we read the results of a study that purports to show a link between a person's astrological sign and profession. Reading further, we discover that the birth dates of a large group of lawyers were examined and more were born under the sign of Leo than under any other sign. Clearly, there is a positive correlation between being a lawyer and being a Leo. This may suggest a causal link between the two factors, but there are at least two plausible explanations for the data that do not involve any sort of causal link between profession and astrological sign. The first is that the correlation is just a coincidence. If we look at a number of groups by profession we may now and then find one where a significantly greater number of people were born under a particular sign, particularly if we restrict our investigation to groups that are none too large. For example, if we do a study of plumbers and their astrological signs and restrict our sample to one or two dozen subjects, chances are quite high we will not find an even distribution under all signs. What we will find is some entirely expectable "clumping": Some signs will have more subjects than others. From here it is but a short step to claim a remarkable correlation between being born under a few astrological signs and becoming a plumber!

The fact that our study only cites one profession and one correlation suggests another possible explanation. It may be that the researchers who undertook the study have presented us with only a small part of their overall data, the part that appears to confirm the possibility of a causal link. Or perhaps, convinced of the truth of astrology, they have inadvertently pruned away just enough data, say by excluding certain subjects, to lend support to the idea of a correlation.

The explanation for a correlation need not be coincidence nor even fudging, inadvertent or otherwise. Frequently, correlations are explained by some third factor that suggests a possible indirect link between two factors. Suppose, for example, that we discover from careful observation of a number of classes that students who sit near the front of the classroom tend to achieve higher grades than students who sit near the rear. This may be a coincidence; at any rate it hardly seems likely that I can improve my grade simply by moving to the front of the classroom. A more likely explanation is that students who want to do well are enthusiastic and want to sit "where the action is," namely near the front of the classroom. Thus it may be that some additional motivational factor accounts for the correlation between the two factors in question.

A concomitant variation between A and B.   Concomitant variation[6] is a convenient name for the second sort of correlation discussed in Chapter 2. It occurs when a variation in one factor, A, is accompanied by a variation in another factor, B. It is quite tempting to conclude that there must be some connection between A and B if changes in the level of one are regularly accompanied by changes in the level of the other. The problem is that an enormous number of entirely unrelated things tend to vary in very regular sorts of ways. For example, over the past ten years there has been a dramatic increase in the popularity of country-western music and a corresponding increase in the cost of a loaf of bread. What is the explanation here? A genuinely baffling causal link? Some overlooked third factor? Most likely we have simply managed to pick two completely unrelated trends that happen to be going in the same direction at the same time.

The fact that A occurs prior to B.   We have all had experiences like this: Just as you think of someone, the phone rings and that person is calling. Recently, a repairer fixed my furnace. A few days later, I noticed that the clock on the thermostat that controls the furnace was not working. It seems natural to conclude that something the repairer did caused the clock to stop, but in such cases the fact that one event precedes another is probably best explained as nothing more than a coincidence. To discount the possibility of coincidence would require some sort of explanation linking the activities of the repairer and the subsequent behavior of the thermostat.

In summary, many kinds of claims are taken to suggest a causal link. Among them are claims about a simple correlation, claims about a concomitant variation, and claims that one thing happened just before another. Although no such claim should be dismissed out of hand, none should be assumed to establish a causal link. The first step in trying to decide whether there is a causal link is to consider possible rival explanations. As our examples suggest, likely candidates are coincidence, inadvertent or deliberate fudging of data, and possible third factors.

Quick Review: Fallacies Involving Rival Explanations

- **False argument by elimination:** Arguing for an explanation by doing nothing more than dismissing possible alternatives. Such arguments often involve the illicit assumption that one of a brief series of possible explanations must be correct.

- **Fallacious causal inference:** Drawing a conclusion about a causal link when the evidence suggests a different explanation. Often overlooked are the possibilities of coincidence, fudging of data, and the influence of other factors.

Fallacies in Proposing and Testing Explanations

Exploiting analogies and similarities. In attempting to explain something puzzling it is sometimes useful to consider a similar thing for which the explanation is well understood. For example, in the late 19th century physicists hypothesized about the existence of what was then called *luminiferous ether*—the medium in which light waves are propagated. They arrived at this notion by thinking of certain similarities between light and sound. Both appear to be wave phenomena; sound waves are propagated in a medium, the atmosphere, much as the waves created by dropping a pebble in a pond are propagated in the surrounding water. Thus physicists reasoned that there must exist a medium for the transmission of light waves as well: a luminiferous ether. Subsequent experimentation, however, demonstrated that there is no such stuff, and so physicists went on to consider other possible explanations for the propagation of light waves. Interestingly enough, physicists next thought about light in terms of another well-understood phenomenon, electromagnetic fields.

This example illustrates the way that thinking about a puzzle in terms of something similar but better understood can lead to possible explanations. But it also illustrates the need for independent testing of explanations arrived at this way. Analogies and similarities are fallaciously exploited when an explanation working in one case is given as evidence for the correctness of a similar explanation in another case. At the very most, a well-chosen similarity guides us to a possible explanation; it should not be thought to provide evidence that the explanation is correct. Only careful testing can provide such evidence.

Consider one explanation often proposed by astrologers. Grant, for the moment, that there is something to astrology and that the position of the stars and planets at the time of our birth can indeed influence our personalities or even our choice of profession. What is the explanation? How is it that the stars and planets influence our lives? Astrologers are likely to give something like the following explanation:

> Much as the moon influences the tides and sunspot activity can disturb radio transmissions, so do the positions of the planets have an important influence on formation of the human personality. Modern science is constantly confirming the interconnectedness of all things. Is it any surprise that distant events, such as the movement of the planets and the decisions people make, should be connected?

So the stars and planets affect our lives much in the way the moon influences the tides. Of course, there is no claim here that the relation between stars and lives is precisely the same as between the moon and the tides or between the sun and radio transmissions. What we have, then, is the barest suggestion that an explanation may be possible for astrological effects and that it may somehow be similar to whatever it is that explains the relation between moon and tides or sun and radio transmissions. We do not have any details of what that explanation might be, but by appealing to something that is understood and suggesting that the explanation for another phenomenon must be similar our astrologer has managed to create the impression that something like an explanation has been given.

Proposing unfalsifiable explanations. To test an explanation we begin by devising a set of experimental conditions by which we predict that something will occur if the explanation is correct. If the predicted result fails to occur, we conclude that the explanation is probably wrong. What this means is that for an explanation to be subject to scientific testing it must in principle be falsifiable. Don't confuse falsifiability with falsehood. Correct explanations as well as incorrect ones are in principle falsifiable, for all it means is that they can be tested as we have described. By contrast, an unfalsifiable explanation would be one whose falsity could not be detected by any conceivable test. It may seem that an unfalsifiable explanation is simply true, but this is not so. An explanation that is in principle unfalsifiable is not a scientific explanation at all. Precisely why this is so can best be explained by an example or two.

A group of people calling themselves "special creationists" claim there is "scientific evidence" that the universe was created by God. Some believe creation occurred only a few thousand years ago; others believe it may have occurred billions of years in the past. Both groups claim, however, that the processes by which God created the world are special in the sense that they are no longer operating in the natural world; the laws of nature by which God created are different from those we currently observe. Very interesting, but what prediction about the world could we make if this claim is true? The process by which God created so quickly and completely are no longer in existence so we should not expect to find evidence of their continuing operation. And for precisely the same reason we should expect to find no evidence against the theory of special creation. It would seem, then, that the creationist explanation is consistent with everything that is happening or could conceivably happen, and so could not possibly be falsified.

But this means that the creationist account is not an explanation at all! To explain something is to try to make clear how or why it happened instead of something else. A proposed explanation that is consistent with what did happen and also with anything else that could have happened explains nothing.

I cashed a large check yesterday and today discovered that it bounced. Looking over my check register, I found a glaring error in addition; I had much less money in my checking account than I thought. My miscalculation, then, explains why my check bounced; had I not miscalculated I would not have written a bad check. Imagine instead I gave this as the explanation: "It must have been fate. What happens, happens." But what if my check had not bounced? Once again I say fate is the reason. Now, it may be that fate determines what we do and do not do. But insofar as the notion of fate is consistent with everything that happens, it cannot be invoked to explain why a particular thing and not something else happened. Maybe fate determined I would bounce a check, maybe not. But by invoking the notion of fate I do not thereby explain why my check bounced as opposed to not bouncing.

We can say something similar about the creationist account of the origin of things. Perhaps God created all things and did so in a very short time using special processes no longer in operation. But by venturing this scenario, the creationist has not explained why things are as they are and not some other way; the scenario is consistent with anything that could conceivably happen. Though the creationist account is interesting it is not a scientific account of things. Does this mean the creationist is wrong? No, but it does mean that special creationism does not constitute a scientific explanation.

So if we find that an apparent explanation cannot be falsified we have uncovered a powerful reason to reject it as an instance of genuine scientific explanation. As a rule of thumb, it is always a good idea to ask of any proposed explanation under what conditions it might be set aside on the grounds that it is false. If no such conditions can be imagined we are dealing at best with fascinating speculation, perhaps even an article of faith, but not a genuine scientific explanation.

Many conspiracy theories seem attractive and plausible largely because they are impervious to falsification. Imagine, for example, that I claim to understand why gasoline prices continue to rise at a much greater rate than the cost of living: There is, sorry to say, a plot, a conspiracy among the major oil companies to ensure that just enough gasoline is refined to keep demand slightly ahead of supply. Might I be wrong, you ask? After all, there have been many congressional investigations of the oil industry and none has yet turned up evidence for such a plot. Well, what do you expect? The one thing we can be sure of in a conspiracy of this magnitude is that the conspirators are going to do everything necessary to cover their tracks, even if it requires buying the services of a few members of Congress. Note here how I have attempted to turn the lack of any evidence against my theory into evidence that it is true. Thus, far from viewing its inability to be falsified as evidence that my theory is not scientific, I take this to be evidence that it must be correct.

A common tactic of conspiracy theorists is to attempt to vindicate their theories by reference to the very facts that have occasioned them. You asked if my theory about the oil companies could be shown to be false. But you didn't ask for my evidence that it is true. That I am on the right track, I might contend, is shown by the fact that if there were such a conspiracy, we would expect gas prices to rise at an artificially high rate. And isn't this just what we find? The problem with this, of course, is that I am using the very facts that have prompted me to give my conspiratorial explanation in an attempt to vindicate it. My thinking is going in a circle. I explain F by reference to T and then claim that F constitutes independent evidence that T is so.

Much of the plausibility of many conspiracy theories stems from the fact that they seem to provide a simple and elegant explanation of a number of apparently unrelated but puzzling facts. So I might go a bit further and point out that because of the oil company conspiracy we see not only artificial rises in oil prices but also lobbyists that represent the entire oil industry, not individual oil companies, in the halls of Congress. Moreover, it explains why a few very influential members of Congress accept large political donations from the oil industry and even why we see so few independent gas stations today—ones not owned the major oil companies. Now a whole series of rather interesting facts are explained by a single conspiracy. Yet in bringing in these additional facts, I am only showing that my theory can be extended to explain a lot. I have yet to provide any evidence that it is true. Though it no doubt sounds intriguing (who among us does not enjoy a good conspiracy?), my theory has yet to be supported by a single independent test.

No doubt there are conspiracies and conspirators, but their existence cannot be proven simply by spinning stories that would if true account for a myriad of interesting facts. One antidote to fallacious conspiracy theories involves considering the possibility of a discrete explanation for each of the facts the theory purportedly explains. It may be, for example, that the reason why members of Congress accept large donations from the oil industry has little to do with the actual explanation for the demise of many independent gas stations.

In addition to conspiracy theories, we should be wary of any attempt to vindicate an explanation by treating known facts as though they were predictive consequences of the explanation. If I know X, I cannot predict X as a means of defending an explanation for X. One evening not too long ago, I passed a person I had never seen before just prior to entering my unlocked office to pick up some tests that needed to be graded. But the tests were missing! My initial hunch was that the stranger had taken the tests. Now, maybe my hunch was right. But suppose someone were to doubt it. I do not provide independent evidence for my explanation by again citing the facts that prompted it, namely the stranger nearby, the unlocked office, and the missing papers.

Claims of extraordinary abilities and events are often made in such a way that they are unfalsifiable. An astrologer claims to be able to tell what awaits us in the future based on our astrological chart. "Expect to move to the East Coast within the next six months," says our astrologer. "However, always remember: the stars impel, they don't compel." Thus the prediction is vindicated if we move east but also if we do not, for we can always choose to change the possible future laid out in our chart. Equally unfalsifiable, though for a different reason, would be this prediction: "You'll be making a significant trip within the next six months." No doubt this is right. I, for one, plan on making an important trip to the bank to deposit a large sum of money to cover my overdraft just as soon as I receive my paycheck. Here our astrologer has guaranteed success not by explaining a possible failed prediction in advance but by making a prediction that is so vague that it will fit an enormous variety of likely events.

Illicit ad hoc rescues.   Explanations and claimed extraordinary abilities need not be dismissed simply because they appear to be false based on a given test. As we said in Chapter 3, it is always worthwhile to consider auxiliary assumptions made in conjunction with a test. It may be that failure is due to a questionable assumption made in setting up the experiment. We might, then, want to modify our test and try again in the event that we fail to get the result we expected. But this sort of holding maneuver can only take us so far. If numerous modifications yield no different results, there is a point at which we must admit that our initial expectations were wrong. To persist in defending our expectations after it is clear they are probably wrong is to engage in what is called an *illicit ad hoc rescue.*

Suppose someone has advanced an explanation but subsequent tests fail to confirm it. The effect of an ad hoc rescue is to suggest a new explanation that explains the failure to confirm the original explanation. Nothing is wrong with such a maneuver provided the new ad hoc explanation can itself be independently tested; it is part and parcel of the way science is done. But such a move is illicit if it is advanced only to save the original explanation by proposing something that, if true, would account for the failure to confirm the original explanation.

The discovery of the planet Neptune provides a good example of the legitimate ad hoc rescue that occurs in scientific research. In the early 1800s six of the seven known planets in our solar system seemed to obey laws set forth by Kepler and Newton. But the outermost planet, Uranus, moved on a considerably different course. Why? One possibility was that the laws in question were a special case capable only of explaining the motions of some of the planets. Another possibility suggested a way for the laws to retain their generality: In the mid-1800s astronomers speculated that the peculiar movement of Uranus could be explained in a way consistent with Newton and Kepler if another planet outside the orbit of Uranus was affecting its movement by gravitational attraction. Now, at this point in the story we must regard the proposed new planet as part of an ad hoc rescue; if there is such a planet the laws in question retain their generality. But astronomers were able to pinpoint where the new planet would have to be to exert the postulated gravitational influence on Uranus, began the search, and shortly thereafter found Neptune precisely where predicted. The ad hoc rescue thus turned out to be justified.

By way of contrast, imagine that a psychic has agreed to be tested and further agrees that he should be able to perform under the experimental conditions we have set up. Instead, he fails the test. Nevertheless, he claims, this does not show that he is not psychic because something called the "shyness effect" causes psychic abilities to ebb and flow—frequently ebbing just when we want them to flow, almost as though they don't want to be tested. It would seem that this appeal to the shyness effect is calculated not to help us rethink our experiment, particularly if there is no independent way of testing for its presence. It is rather nothing more than an attempt to make sure that no matter how carefully we design our experimental test no conceivable result need be taken as repudiating the psychic's claimed ability. By contrast with the legitimate ad hoc rescue that ended in the discovery of Neptune, our psychic's maneuver seems clearly to constitute an illicit ad hoc rescue. It would appear to be untestable and its only redeeming feature is that, if true, it would save our psychic in the face of his failure to perform under controlled conditions.

> ## Quick Review: Fallacies in Proposing and Testing Explanations
>
> ■ **Exploiting analogies and similarities:** Defending a novel explanation by emphasizing its similarity to a more well-established explanation
>
> ■ **Unfalsifiable explanation:** An explanation that is consistent with anything and everything that could occur
>
> ■ **Unfalsifiable predictions:** A prediction so broad or vague that it will come to pass no matter what happens
>
> ■ **Conflating initiating facts with predictions:** Using as a prediction that which is known to be true, namely the very facts that have occasioned the explanation at issue
>
> ■ **Illicit ad hoc rescues:** Inventing auxiliary assumptions simply as a means of explaining away a failed prediction and with little regard for whether the assumptions are plausible or testable

■
___

SCIENCE AND PSEUDOSCIENCE

All of the ways by which scientific inquiry can go astray that we have considered suggest a problem. How do we determine whether a result advanced in the name of science is genuine or bogus? Our discussion of fallacious uses of the methods of science suggests one crucial difference between genuine science on the one hand and pseudoscience—fake science—on the other. Genuine science involves the rigorous testing of new ideas; as such, the results of a genuine scientific investigation will employ the methods introduced in Chapters 2 through 4. Pseudoscientific ideas will frequently be backed by evidence that is the product of one or more of the fallacies discussed in this chapter. Though adherence to the methods of science is at the heart of the distinction between genuine and pseudoscience, there are a number of other important differences between the two as well as a number of mistaken ideas about what the distinction involves.

Science cannot be distinguished from pseudoscience on the basis of the quality of the results each produces. In science, ideas earn their respectability not because they are right but because they are tested in the right way. Many of the examples we have considered here and in preceding chapters serve to confirm this. At one point in the history of Western thought the best informed scientific view was that the earth is at the center of the universe. Though this view was ultimately shown to be wrong, it constituted the best science of the time; though Ptolemy and his followers were mistaken, their view of the cosmos provided a coherent, testable explanation for a wide variety of phenomena. Our discussion earlier in this chapter of the luminiferous ether provides another striking example of genuine though ultimately mistaken science.

The distinction between science and pseudoscience cannot be drawn along lines of scientific discipline. We cannot say, for example, that astronomy is a science but astrology is not, that psychology is but psychic research isn't. This is not to say that astronomy or psychology do not deserve to be called a science. But the notion of science or scientific discipline is much too broad for our purposes. My dictionary defines astronomy as "the science which treats of the heavenly bodies—stars, planets, satellites and comets," and I suppose this is as good a definition as any. But within this broad discipline we sometimes encounter instances of pseudoscience as well as of genuine science.

For example, in the 1950s a self-proclaimed astronomer and archeologist, Immanuel Velikovsky, hypothesized that the planet Venus was created out of an enormous volcanic eruption on Jupiter. He speculated that as the newly formed planet hurtled toward the sun it passed by the earth, causing several cataclysmic events, and eventually settled down to become the second planet in our solar system. Yet careful examination of Velikovsky's work has shown that the sort of cosmic ping-pong involved is quite impossible and that he either ignored or was unaware of certain physical constraints that his hypothesis violated. One of Velikovsky's most glaring mistakes involves a well-known law of motion: If one body exerts a force on a second body, the second exerts a force that is equal in strength and opposite in direction. An explosion of sufficient magnitude to allow an object the size of Venus to overcome the gravitational attraction of Jupiter would simultaneously send Jupiter off in the opposite direction, despite Jupiter's great mass. Yet in Velikovsky's theory the orbit of Jupiter remains unaffected by this most cataclysmic of events. Here, then, we have an example of pseudoscience that we can certainly classify under the broad heading of astronomy.

Similarly, early in this century British psychologist Sir Cyril Burt claimed to have decisive evidence that heredity, not environment, plays the dominant role in determining intelligence. As it turned out, much of Burt's work was based on fictional or distorted data. Burt apparently invented experimental subjects and altered test results to conform to his expectations in the process of trying to make his findings appear to be scientific.

The distinction between science and pseudoscience has nothing to do with the distinction between "hard" and "soft" science. The sciences that study human behavior—sociology, anthropology, psychology, and political science, to name a few—are sometimes characterized as "soft" as opposed to the "hard" physical and biological sciences. Though in a number of respects the soft and hard sciences differ, none of the differences are sufficient to support the complaint occasionally leveled against the soft disciplines that they are pseudosciences. The hard sciences do not have to deal with the complexities posed by the human ability to choose what to do in their attempts at describing and understanding nature. Physicists and chemists, for example, do not have to worry about the Hawthorne effect in their research. It is sometimes said that only the hard sciences are exact, which is generally taken to mean that predictions about human behavior cannot hope to be as precise as, say, predictions about what will happen to a gas under a specific set of conditions. Moreover, it is difficult to think of a single soft-science theory that is as broad in scope as the theories of modern physics and chemistry. The law of gravity describes the behavior of all gravitating objects; it is hard to imagine a similar law describing a single aspect of the behavior of people, societies, or economic or political institutions.

Yet despite their obvious differences, the hard and soft sciences are all proper sciences: All aim at explaining phenomena of the natural world, be it the behavior of matter or of human beings. And both hard and soft sciences adhere to the methods we discussed in Chapters 2 through 4 in advancing and testing their hows and whys. Many philosophers argue that the social sciences will never produce the kinds of grand, unifying theories characteristic of the physical and biological sciences; it may be that the soft sciences will have to be satisfied with discrete bits of explanatory material, each suited to a limited aspect of human behavior. But insofar as research in the social and behavioral sciences conforms to the more general methods of good scientific research, we have no reason to doubt their qualifications as disciplines capable of delivering genuine scientific results.

Genuine science tends to be self-correcting; pseudoscience does not. We have examined a number of instances in which the results of scientific inquiry have been overturned, most often on the basis of further scientific inquiry. It is estimated that there are currently about 40,000 active scientific journals worldwide. They contain detailed synopses of research projects, generally written by those who have done the research. An article reporting on new research will contain a description of the design and results of the experiment, discussion of the significance of the results, and suggestions for future research. Most journals are "refereed": Submitted articles are reviewed by other scientists who check to make sure the article is accurate and complete. The referees finally decide whether the research described in the article is sufficiently interesting and important to merit publication. It is not unusual for a submitted manuscript to be returned to its author or authors for substantial revision. Thus the process by which journals decide what to accept and reject serves to correct numerous potential errors.

This process is far from perfect. Given the sheer number of journals and articles, mistakes are bound to go unnoticed, some of them pretty spectacular. In the past few years, several instances have surfaced of published research that involved fabricated data. Fortunately such incidents are fairly rare.[7] The fact that they have been discovered is itself testimony to the self-correcting tendency of the process by which research is made public. When fraudulent research is detected it is usually by other scientists—peers who have taken the time to look carefully at the published results.

Scientific journals serve another function as well: They provide a forum for critics of current research. Often journals publish articles mounting objections to and uncovering flaws in previously reported research. Since the early 1980s, for example, an enormous amount of research has been directed at understanding AIDS and its cause or causes. The vast majority of AIDS research points to a retrovirus—the human immunodeficiency virus (HIV)—as the cause of AIDS. This contention has emerged from thousands of experiments and clinical trials both on animals and humans undertaken by medical doctors, biologists, geneticists, and specialists in other related disciplines. Yet a handful of AIDS researchers, notably Peter Duesberg, a professor of molecular and cell biology, and Robert Root-Bernstein, a professor of physiology, have mounted serious objections to the mainstream view. Duesberg argues that a careful analysis of the evidence strongly suggests that AIDS is not caused by HIV, Root-Bernstein that HIV is but one of several cofactors that must be present for AIDS to develop. Both have suggested that much of the research into AIDS and its causes undertaken in the last 20 years has been largely misdirected. As you might suspect, the work of Duesberg and Root-Bernstein has met with a great deal of resistance from the vast majority of AIDS researchers; in the last few years many articles have appeared in the scientific literature that are highly critical of their methodology and findings.[8]

This episode illustrates several of the reasons why science stands a good chance of correcting its own mistakes. First, the research criticized by Duesberg and Root-Bernstein was readily available in the form of published articles in scientific journals. Second, both are credentialed, mainstream researchers. Third, the critiques produced by them were taken sufficiently seriously to be published in reputable scientific journals; Duesberg's work, for example, has appeared in *Science* and *Nature*, two of the most visible and highly respected scientific journals. Finally, their criticisms were not simply dismissed on the grounds that they were out of step with mainstream views. Other scientists have taken them seriously enough to devote considerable time and space to rebuttals, again in the forum provided by scientific publications.

Interestingly enough, most criticism of potentially pseudoscientific research comes from within mainstream science as well. Recent criticism of the work of the special creationists, for example, has been leveled by mainstream anthropologists, zoologists, biologists, and evolutionary theorists. Though there are a small number of journals devoted to creationist science, it is rare to find a single article by a noted creationist critical of the work of other creationists.

As a scientific discipline develops it will gradually produce a maturing body of explanatory or theoretical findings; pseudoscience produces very little theory. One major aim of science, as we discussed in Chapter 1, is to make sense of nature by providing better and better and often more and more encompassing bodies of explanatory material. Think, for example, of all that is known about the mechanisms involved in the transmission of genetic information from one generation to the next by contrast with what was known 150 years ago at the birth of the science of genetics. Gregor Mendel, the first great figure in the field of genetic research, began by speculating about "genetic factors" that might be responsible for observable characteristics in some simple varieties of plants. Today, modern geneticists speak of the subtle and complex methods by which DNA is transmitted in any organism.

By contrast, pseudoscientific research almost always produces spectacular claims for extraordinary abilities and events, but little else. Moreover, the nature of the claims produced varies little over time. As it turns out, ESP research began only a little later than genetic research. Yet today we find little more than an enormous body of controversial evidence that a few people have psychic ability and almost no theoretical understanding of how ESP might work. What little explanatory material emerges in many pseudoscientific endeavors is likely to be based on vague analogies and similarities drawn from some well-understood area of science. For example, a book on ESP published in the 1930s was entitled *ESP: Mental Radio*. An interesting idea, but hardly a reliable explanation.

The findings, theoretical and otherwise, of genuine science are always open to revision; rarely do pseudoscientific claims change much over time. It is hard to imagine a thriving scientific discipline today wherein much of what was believed 100 or even 50 years ago has not been supplanted by a more accurate picture of things. Fifty years ago particle physics provided us with a picture of the world in which the most fundamental particles were the electron, proton, and neutron. A few stray experimental results were in conflict with this picture, but few physicists questioned its rough fit with reality. Today physics provides a more comprehensive picture in which protons and neutrons are composites built out of more fundamental particles, quarks. The landscape of the particle physicists has changed dramatically in a brief period of time.

The openness of science to revision does not mean that scientific results cannot achieve a kind of permanence. Many of the findings of science will doubtless not be repudiated by new research. Science will not discover that water molecules are composed of something other than two atoms of hydrogen and one of oxygen; no one doubts that Newton was correct in seeing that gravitational attraction is directly proportional to mass and inversely proportional to distance. The changes we can anticipate in well-established areas of science generally occur at the level of underlying explanation: Why do gravitating objects behave in the way Newton discovered? What is the internal structure of the stuff water is made of? And just how, if at all, are the forces at work inside the atom connected to the force responsible for gravity?

By way of contrast, it is interesting to look at the work of modern astrologers. If you were to have a competent astrologer draw a detailed horoscope, his or her work would be based on classic astrological texts written nearly 2000 years ago. Pseudoscientists often claim the long history of their ideas to be evidence for their correctness. Thus an astrologer might boast that his or her techniques are derived from the discoveries of ancient Babylonian and Egyptian astronomers. In and of itself this is not reason to classify astrology as a pseudoscience, but at the level of underlying explanation astrology remains today in much the position it was at its inception. After 2000 years astrologers have conspicuously failed to produce even the beginnings of a plausible explanation for its purported effects. Conspicuously missing in the history of astrological research is any evidence of the kind of proposing, testing, modifying, and revising of new ideas that typifies scientific progress.

Genuine science embraces skepticism; pseudoscience tends to view skepticism as a sign of narrow-mindedness. The first reaction of a competent scientist when faced with something new and unusual is to try to explain it away by fitting it into what is already known. Many people who engage in pseudoscience see this as the worst sort of skepticism; the fact that one's initial reaction is to try to rob something of its mystery is taken to be a sign that one is unwilling to entertain new ideas. It is perhaps this attitude toward scientific skepticism more than anything else that contributes to the tendency in pseudoscience to accept claims in the absence of solid scientific evidence.

The question of whether a piece of scientific research is genuine or bogus is not always easy to answer. Though the eight points of contrast we have made can provide us with some initial sense of when we are in the presence of pseudoscience, we should not wield them dogmatically. If someone purports to have scientific evidence for something, we should not dismiss their work simply because they refuse to countenance serious criticism, complain that their critics lack an open mind, or proclaim the longevity of their ideas. Rather, such moves should only be taken as a sign that something may well be seriously amiss. The fundamental difference between genuine science and bogus science is really one of method. The results of genuine scientific inquiry are the product of open and honest applications of the methods we have discussed in previous chapters. Pseudoscientific results, by contrast, are produced with little regard for these methods.

A person claims to have scientific evidence for X. Are we confronted with genuine science or pseudoscience? To answer, there is no substitute for taking a careful, critical look at the methods employed in establishing X.

■
_____

THE LIMITS OF SCIENTIFIC EXPLANATION

In Chapter 1 we said that one major goal of science is to further our understanding of how and why things happen as they do. In Chapters 2 through 5 we have taken a close look at the method by which science attempts to accomplish this goal and at some of the ways the methods of science can be abused. One issue, however, deserves brief discussion before we conclude: Are there hows and whys that science cannot help answer? In other words, are there things that science is powerless to explain?

With respect to questions about processes occurring in the natural world, it is hard to imagine a limit to the potential of science to explain. This does not mean that given enough time and effort science will provide us with an understanding of all natural processes, only that there appears to be no limit to the questions about the natural world that science, properly carried out, can profitably address. And if it turns out there are such limits, we will discover them only by approaching them scientifically and discovering just how far this approach can carry us.

But there other hows and other whys that take us beyond the interests we normally associate with scientific inquiry. These are the great questions of metaphysics, questions that have vexed philosophers and ordinary people alike for as long as people have thought. They are questions you have probably wondered about in some idle moment: Why is there anything at all, rather than nothing? Is there some benevolent, creative force responsible for the natural world? Is there, in other words, a God? Why are we here? Do our lives have some ultimate meaning, some cosmic purpose?

Deep metaphysical questions like these, I suspect, will not be settled by scientific inquiry. Not that science is somehow deficient; its methods simply are not designed to answer questions of this sort. Science aims to explain processes occurring within the natural world. By contrast, deep metaphysical questions raise issues about the nature of the natural world itself. They are not concerned with mechanisms, causes, laws—the very stuff of scientific explanation. Rather they involve an attempt to understand the purposes behind the sum total of the natural world. If scientific questions are by definition about how and why things happen in the natural world, metaphysical questions are by definition not scientific. Even if science were somehow, someday to provide us with an utterly complete explanatory picture of all processes in nature—a theory of everything—it would leave our deep metaphysical questions untouched. Why this particular set of explanations and not another? What is their cosmic significance? Their purpose? Who is their author?

Not long before his death, Sir Peter Medawar, Nobel laureate in medicine, made the following observation:

> Catastrophe apart, I believe it to be science's greatest glory that there is no limit upon the power of science to answer questions of the kind science can answer.[9]

Metaphysical questions aside, there would seem to be no limit upon the ability of science to explain so long as we restrict science to the kind of question, as Medawar says, that science can answer.

■
___

SUMMARY

Here is a brief summary of the fallacies we have discussed and of the tell-tale signs of pseudoscience.

Fallacies in Scientific Reasoning

    Fallacies involving initial observations

        Anecdotal evidence: basing a general claim on a few anecdotal reports

        Omitting facts: creating an air of mystery by leaving facts that might account for the mystery

Distorting the facts: altering the facts to create the impression that something is mysterious

Fallacies involving rival explanations

Fallacious argument by elimination: arguing for a given explanation by attempting to show that rival explanations are wrong

Fallacious inference to a causal link: inferring a causal link on the basis of a correlation, concomitant variation, or the fact that the suspected cause occurred before its effect. Possible rival explanations are coincidence, fudging of data, and third factors.

Fallacies in proposing and testing explanations

Exploiting analogies and similarities: treating explanations for well-understood phenomena as though they were evidence for a similar explanation for something not so well understood

Proposing unfalsifiable claims: (1) advancing a claim, explanatory or otherwise, that is consistent with everything that could happen; (2) working with predictions that cannot be falsified; (3) explaining away all conceivable experimental results that might suggest that a claim is false; or (4) treating initiating facts as confirming facts

Illicit ad hoc rescues: advancing auxiliary assumptions that cannot be independently verified as a means of saving an explanation or extraordinary claim

The Tell-Tale Signs of Pseudoscience

1. Pseudoscientific claims often involve fallacious scientific reasoning of the sort exemplified by the fallacies just described.

2. Pseudoscience can occur within the bounds of legitimate scientific disciplines.

3. Pseudoscience tends not to be self-correcting. *peer reviewed. scientists correct ea. others publica*

4. Pseudoscience produces very little explanatory theory. *tends to introduce little facts, but no larger body of fact.*

5. Rarely do pseudoscientific claims change much over time; pseudoscientists take this fact to be a scientific virtue. *real science accumulates, or overthrows theories, pseudo science doesn't change.*

6. Pseudoscientists tend to view skepticism as a sign of narrow-mindedness.

real science relies on skepticism.

■
_____

EXERCISES

Many of the following passages involve one or more of the fallacies we have discussed. Comment on any fallacies you find; name them and explain in more detail how each involves the fallacy or fallacies you have uncovered. When appropriate, speculate about rival explanations that have been overlooked. Be on the lookout for examples of the other characteristic features of pseudoscience and comment on any you find. Problems you will encounter in some of the passages will be difficult to classify, and in thinking about mistakes they may involve you will need to rely on your by now well-developed sense of what good scientific research involves. In other words, you may need to apply some of the ideas presented in Chapters 2 through 4. (Note: A solution to Exercise 1 is provided on page 145.)

1. A remarkable fact is that many of the great scientists and mathematicians in history have had a deep interest in music. Einstein, for example, was a devoted amateur violinist and Newton is said to have been fascinated by the mathematical structure of musical compositions. If you want your child to pursue a career in science, you would be well advised to do everything you can to develop his or her interest in music.

2. The following is excerpted from an article in the *Weekly World News* entitled "First Photo of a Human Soul":

    What was expected to be a routine heart surgery wound up making religious and medical history when a photographer snapped a picture of the patient's body a split second after she died. The dramatic photo clearly shows a glowing angelic spirit rising up off the operating table as the line of Karin Fisher's heart monitor went flat at the moment of death. And while nobody in the operating theater actually saw the strange entity as it left the 32-year-old patient's body, scholars, clergymen and the Vatican itself are hailing the photo as the most dramatic proof of life after death ever.

    "This is it. This is the proof that true believers the world over have been waiting for," Dr. Martin Muller, who has conducted an extensive study of the picture, told reporters.

    Oddly enough, not one of the 12 doctors, nurses and technicians in the operating room saw the glowing spirit leave the woman's body, apparently because it wasn't visible to the naked eye.

    But as a matter of routine the procedure was photographed by the hospital's director of education, Peter Valentin, who found a single black and white picture of the spirit among 72 prints that were made.

    "The photo has been the focus of intense study and debate for several weeks now and the consensus of both scholars and clergymen is that it is indeed authentic," said Dr. Muller.

"That's not to say that there aren't any skeptics because there are," he continued. "The problem with their position is that they can offer no alternative explanations for the flowing image that turned up on the picture. In fact, there are no alternative explanations. You either accept the image in faith, as I do, or you reject it. There is no in-between."[10]

3. Acupuncture has been practiced in Asia for nearly 3000 years. It is based on the belief that the mind and body are a continuum, a self-contained bioelectric system through which runs a river of energy called *qi* or *ch'i*. Two opposite currents flow in this river, yin (night, dark, cold, female) and yang (day, light, hot, male), and well-being requires that they be balanced. Illness and pain occur when they are not, when metabolic waste and energy back up at the site of an injury. By using hair-thin needles, a burning herb called moxa that heats the inserted needle to intensify its stimulation, and on very rare occasions electrodes, acupuncturists are able to regulate the flow of the qi through 12 channels called meridians. To do so, they place needles at any one or several of the 2000 named points that correspond to the body's muscles, organs, and systems.

4. Graphologists claim to be able to tell a great deal about people from their handwriting. The following is from a report prepared for the author by a professional graphologist:

You are a person who is alive to the world about you and you react quickly, and in a friendly way to those who show you a friendly interest. You are easily influenced by life's many joys and sorrows, and your first response to any situation in life, pleasant or unpleasant, will be an emotionally responsive one. Even though you are strongly influenced by the way you feel, you will not go to extremes and allow your emotions to rule your life by controlling you entirely.

5. You have probably heard about *back masking*—inserting subliminal messages in recordings of popular music in reverse. Some people claim that if you play such recordings backward you can actually hear the message. But have you ever wondered how the mind deciphers the message when it is heard backward? Well, the answer is quite simple. We do not hear individual words when we listen to speech or lyrics. Instead we hear whole sentences constructed of individual words like a chain of linked metal loops. Whole sentences can be processed by the brain either forward or backward, much as a linked chain can be dragged back and forth.

6. Though most reports of UFOs can be explained in perfectly ordinary ways—as sightings of weather balloons, blimps, the moon, or the like—there remains a small residue of cases that has no known explanation. These sightings are typically by reliable people and are often reported by a number of ob-

servers. Thus we can rule out the possibility of a hoax of some sort. It seems clear then that we have evidence that earth has been visited by beings from another planet or star system.

7. The following passage is from an article in *IMPACT*, a publication of the Institute for Creation Research, entitled "Modern Scientific Discovery Verifies the Scriptures."

If there is a second law of thermodynamics, there must be a first law, of course. Indeed there is, and this natural law confirms another scientifically testable statement found in the Bible. The First Law of Thermodynamics states that the total quantity of energy and matter in the universe is a constant. One form of energy may be converted into another, energy may be converted into matter, and matter may be converted into energy, but the total quantity always remains the same. The First Law of Thermodynamics, the most firmly established law in natural science, confirms the Biblical statement concerning a finished creation, as found in Genesis 2:1.2: "Thus the heavens and the earth were finished, and all the host of them. And on the seventh day God ended His work which He has made; and He rested on the seventh day from all His work which He had made." If it could be shown that somewhere in this universe matter or energy was coming into being from nothing, then this Biblical statement of a finished creation would be falsified. The opposite is true. It has been precisely verified. Once again, a Biblical statement has withstood scientific test.

8. Is it just a coincidence that there are so many parallels between the lives of famous people living at different times? Perhaps. But perhaps not. It may be that we have lived past lives and that certain of our traits persist from lifetime to lifetime. You are no doubt aware of some of the eerie similarities between John F. Kennedy and Abraham Lincoln. This is only the tip of the iceberg. Consider the strange parallels between the lives of George Washington and Dwight Eisenhower:

   1. Both came to prominence as victorious generals.

   2. Both served two full terms as president.

   3. Both gave famous farewell speeches warning the United States against foolish military policies.

   4. Both were replaced as president by Harvard graduates named John from wealthy, prominent Massachusetts families.

   5. "Eisenhower" and "Washington" have ten letters each.

   6. "Dwight" and "George" have six letters each.

   7. Neither belonged to a political party before seeking the presidency.

9. "What goes around comes around." In this simple statement lies one of the most profound truths about human destiny, sometimes called the Law of Karma. Even the Bible recognizes this most fundamental of truths: "As ye sow, so shall ye reap." You may think there are bound to be exceptions to this cosmic law of justice. After all, people do not always suffer the consequences of the bad things they do nor are they consistently rewarded for the good. But have faith. The results of our actions may not catch up with us in this life, but there are other lives. What we sow in this existence we may reap in another incarnation.

10. A recent study of 50 of America's most profitable companies revealed some interesting facts. Many of the companies have resisted the temptation to expand into new and unfamiliar industries. As Robert W. Johnson, former chairman of Johnson and Johnson, put it, "Never acquire a business you don't know how to run." It seems clear that the odds increase that a large company will remain profitable over the long haul if it sticks to doing business in areas with which it is familiar.

11. Some psychics claim to be able to help the police, usually with cases involving missing persons or unsolved murders. These "psychic detectives" claim that they work with police departments as consultants on many unsolved cases. Typically a psychic goes to the scene of a crime or the place where a person was last seen and uses ESP to "see" important facts pertaining to the case. Actually the police very rarely initiate a request for help from a psychic. In most cases, the parents or relatives of a missing or dead person contact a psychic, pay for his or her help, and then offer the findings to the police.

12. A recent study suggests that near-death experiences may have a physiological or psychological explanation. In the study, the medical records of 100 patients who would have died without medical intervention were compared with those of another 100 patients who were not in danger of dying but thought they were. The researchers discovered that about the same number of subjects in each group—32 in the first group and 35 in the second—reported having near-death experiences. I think we must take the results of this study with a grain of salt. It may be that the people who mistakenly believed they were near death somehow inadvertently triggered the psychological or physiological mechanism by which the soul leaves the body. Thus though they mistakenly believed they were near death their near-death experiences were nonetheless genuine.

Exercises 13–15 are all taken from Bio-Rhythm: A Personal Science.[11] Biorhythm is the notion that from birth to death each of us is influenced by three internal cycles—the physical, the emotional, and the intellectual.

13. On the evening of November 11, 1960, a retired Swiss importer named George Thommen was interviewed on the "Long John Nebel Show," a radio talkathon based in New York City. What Thommen had to say sounded surprising to most people and incredible to some. However, the strangest thing Thommen said was in the form of a warning. He cautioned that Clark Gable, who was then in the hospital recovering from a heart attack suffered six days before while filming *The Misfits* with Marilyn Monroe, would have to be very careful on November 16. On that date, explained Thommen, Gable's "physical rhythm" would be "critical." As a result, his condition would be unstable, putting him in danger of a relapse.

    Few listeners took Thommen's warning seriously. Gable and his doctors were probably unaware of it. On Wednesday, November 16, 1960, Clark Gable suffered an unexpected second heart attack and died. His doctor later admitted that his life might have been saved if the needed medical equipment had been in place beside his bed when he was stricken a second time.

14. Actually, the theory of biorhythm is little more than an extension and generalization of the enormous amount of research that scientists have already done on the many biological rhythms and cycles of life. From the migration of swallows and the feeding patterns of oysters to the levels of hormones in human blood and the patterns of sleep, life can be defined as regulated time. Countless rhythms, most of them fairly predictable, can be found in even the simplest of our bodily functions. Even the smallest component of our bodies, the cell, follows several clearly defined cycles as it creates and uses up energy.

15. There is nothing in biorhythm theory that contradicts scientific knowledge. . . . But until we can perform strictly controlled studies of how and why biorhythm works and until many other researchers have been able to replicate these studies, we will have to base the case for biorhythm on purely empirical research. . . . Ultimately, however, the most convincing studies of biorhythm are those you can do yourself. By working out your own biorhythm chart and biorhythm profiles for particular days, and then comparing them with your experiences of up and down days, of illness and health, of success and failure, you will be able to judge for yourself.

16. Sociobiology is the theory that the major component of social behavior is biological adaptation. In the view of many sociobiologists, the structure of human and animal societies are determined in large measure by the innate biological impulse to increase their chances of survival as species. One large difficulty faced by the sociobiologist is the existence of social arrangements that appear to be of little adaptive value yet appear to occur in all human cultures. Why, for example, are there a significant number of homosexuals in all cultures, given that procreation is necessary for survival? One sociobiologist has suggested that in primitive societies homosexuals were free of pa-

rental obligations and so could help their close relatives with unrivaled efficiency. If they succeeded, their relatives would produce more children, thus passing on their genes to the next generation. Similarly, religions may have developed in many human cultures as a means of giving their members a driving purpose that would motivate a desire to survive and to pass wisdom to future generations.

17. For years stories have been circulating about an internal combustion engine invented sometime in the 1950s that burns a simple combination of hydrogen and oxygen instead of gasoline. This "water engine," as it is sometimes called, could revolutionize the world economy by freeing us of our dependence on fossil fuels and making transportation virtually free to everyone. But don't hold your breath. The major players in the global economy are a tight confederation of industries and countries involved in the manufacture, maintenance, and fueling of automobiles. So enormous is the global monetary investment in the status quo that it is virtually impossible that the water engine will ever see the light of day. The major oil and automotive companies have seen to it that all patents pertaining to this revolutionary new invention are under their control and have orchestrated the suppression of all information about it out of fear that it would, if marketed, cost them billions of dollars. Ask any representative of the oil or automotive industry—or any government official for that matter—about the water engine and I predict this is just what you will hear: either "no comment" or "there's simply no such thing."

18. You don't think there is anything to astrology? Well, consider this. Last week, I was at a meeting of the local chapter of the American Philosophical Association. Only about 50 philosophers were at the meeting, yet three were born on the same day of the year and two other pairs of philosophers had identical birth dates!

19. The following newspaper article appeared under the heading "Ex-USO Professor Theorizes About Alien Beings":

Aliens from distant worlds may be watching earth and making unofficial contact with selected humans, says a recently retired scientist at Oregon State University. His theory is that advanced and benevolent space beings may have adopted an embargo on official contact with earthlings, wishing to avoid the chaos that could sweep the planet if their presence were suddenly revealed.

Instead, they have adopted a "leaky embargo" policy that allows contact only with citizens whose stories are unlikely to be credible to scientists and the government, said the scientist, James W. Deardorff, 58, professor emeritus of atmospheric sciences.

"They just want to let those know who are prepared to accept it in their minds that there are other beings," Deardorff said. "They may want to slowly prepare us for the shock that could come later when they reveal themselves. . . ."

Deardorff is prepared to accept many ideas looked upon skeptically by other scientists, including telepathy and the possibility of time travel and physical dimensions other than space and time.

His open-mindedness has made it more difficult to operate in the scientific mainstream, where scientific committees have been formed to debunk theories about UFOs and psychic phenomena.

"There's a lot of polarization going on now," he said, adding that he has had trouble getting some papers on extraterrestrials published in scientific journals. "There's a lot less middle ground than there used to be," he said. "It's no accident that I'm getting more active in this area now after retirement."[12]

20. I have a new theory about that most mysterious of forces, gravity. Though physicists can describe for us the laws gravity follows, they have failed entirely to explain the mechanism by which it works. I think I have the answer: Every massive object in the universe generates invisible, spring-like tendrils in the direction of every other object in its immediate vicinity. When these tendrils connect, they function like a coiled spring, with the tension varying in direct proportion to the product of the masses of the objects they connect and in inverse proportion to the square of the distance between the objects. I call these tendrils "virtual springs." Thus, virtual springs grow in strength as objects are closer together and weaken as objects recede from one another. That I am on to something remarkable is suggested by the fact that if my theory is right objects of differing masses should all accelerate toward another massive object, say the surface of the earth, and moreover should do so at roughly the same rate. By careful experimentation I have established the truth of both these predictions: All massive objects do tend to fall toward the earth and at precisely the same rate of acceleration irrespective of mass!

21. Telekinesis is the ability to bring about physical changes by purely mental processes. Is telekinesis real? Consider the following experiment. A computer is programmed to generate numbers at random. When an odd number is generated the computer prints out "odd," and when an even number is generated it prints out "even." Prior to the generation of each number, the experimenter instructs the experimental subject to think "odd" or "even" and to mark down the choice on a tally sheet. The experimenter then instructs the computer to generate a number and the result is tallied against the choice of the subject. Several hundred trials are run. Under these conditions it is predicted that subjects with telekinetic ability will score much higher than chance would predict—that is, the computer and the experimental subject will agree more than 50% of the time.

22. Recently I carried out a telepathy experiment on 50 of my students. I shuffled a standard deck of playing cards. Sitting behind a screen that blocked me from my subject's line of sight, I turned over the cards one at a time. I concentrated on the value of the card—ace, three, king, or whatever—and then instructed the subjects to record what they thought the card was. I did this for the entire deck. We would expect them to get about 8% right, or about 1 out of 13, by sheer chance, because there are 13 possible values for a card. And indeed none of my subjects scored much higher or lower than this. But that is not the end of the story. Close analysis of the results shows that several students were within two cards of the card I was concentrating on nearly half the time! It seems clear to me that these subjects have demonstrated at least some ability to pick up thoughts telepathically.

23. From a flyer advertising a chiropractic clinic:

Ronald Pero, Ph.D., researched the immune system at the University of Lund Medical School, Lund, Sweden, and the Preventative Medical Institute, New York City. He measured both immune resistance to disease and the ability to repair genetic damage.

In a news report about his study in *East/West Journal*, November 1989, chiropractic patients were compared to two groups: normal, healthy people and cancer patients. The chiropractic patients were all in long term care on a wellness basis. Their immune function was measured to be two times stronger than the healthy people, and four times stronger than the sick! And this increase occurred regardless of age. With ongoing chiropractic care, the immune system does not deteriorate, as in other groups.

24. From an ad for past life drawings—drawings by a psychic of the way we looked in our past lives:

Since I've been doing Past Life Drawings and Readings for people, I'm often amazed at how relevant the information is in their present lives. Even though we may have had thousands of incarnations, I've found that there are usually three main past lives which are influencing our present lives the most.

One woman that I did drawings for had a past life in India as a young male who rode and trained elephants to lift logs and move stones to build a temple. Years later when the temple was completed, the man decided to spend the rest of his life meditating in the temple. The woman revealed that she had been doing Eastern meditation for many years and she also had a large ceramic elephant lamp, elephant bookends and other elephant figurines all around the house.

One man had an unpleasant life on a ship which ended when he was tied and thrown overboard into the ocean and drowned. The man had always been afraid of water in this life and never learned to swim. I worked with this man to bring the drowning experience into the present time and helped him to release the emotions and fear connected with it. A month later he was swimming and inner-tubing in Timothy Lake with his wife and sons.

25. Many strange and wonderful things are attributed to the mysterious power of the pyramid. For example, you can increase the life of a razor blade by keeping it stored inside a simple plastic pyramid. If you don't believe me, try this simple experiment. After you use your razor, remove the blade, wash it in warm water and then dry the blade off. Finally, place it inside or under a small pyramid-shaped container. I think you will be surprised at how long the blade retains its sharpness.

26. If you are wondering how pyramids manage to accomplish this marvelous feat, consider the following explanation by G. Patrick Flannigen, self-proclaimed pyramid power expert: The shape of the pyramid acts as a sort of lens or focus for the transmission of biocosmic energy.

27. I've had it with my local supermarket. Every time I shop there it seems it's out of something I need. Only yesterday I stopped to pick up a cantaloupe on my way home and, wouldn't you know, it was out. And just last week it was out of the ice cream that was on sale. I'm going to start shopping somewhere that does a better job of managing inventory.

28. A recent study has shown that on average a graduate of an ivy league college will make more money over the course of his or her career than a graduate of any other college. Moreover, a graduate of an East Coast college will make more than a graduate of a midwestern, southern, or western college. It seems clear that if you want to make it financially, you ought to try to get into an ivy league school or, if you can't, at least into a college on the East Coast.

29. The following newspaper story appeared under the headline "Gyroscope Test Possibly Defies Gravity":

Japanese scientists have reported that small gyroscopes lose weight when spun under certain conditions, apparently in defiance of gravity. If proved correct, the finding would mark a stunning scientific advance, but experts said they doubted that it would survive intense scrutiny.
   A systematic way to negate gravitation, the attraction between all masses and particles of matter in the universe, has eluded scientists since the principles of the force were first elucidated by Isaac Newton in the 17th century. The anti-gravity work is reported in the Dec. 18, 1989 issue of Physical Review Letters, which is regarded by experts as one of the world's leading journals of physics and allied fields. Its articles are rigorously reviewed by other scientists before being accepted for publication, and it rejects far more than it accepts.

Experts who have seen the report said that it seemed to be based on sound research and appeared to have no obvious sources of experimental error, but they cautioned that other seemingly reliable reports have collapsed under close examination.

The work was performed by Hideo Hayasaka and Sakae Takeuchi of the engineering faculty at Tohoku University in Sendai, Japan.

Unlike the exaggerated claims made for low-temperature or "cold" nuclear fusion this year, the current results are presented with scientific understatement. The authors do not claim to have defied gravity, but simply say their results "cannot be explained by the usual theories."

"It's an astounding claim," said Robert L. Park, a professor of physics at the University of Maryland who is director of the Washington office of the American Physical Society, which publishes Physical Review Letters. "It would be revolutionary if true. But it's almost certainly wrong. Almost all extraordinary claims are wrong."

The experiment looked at weight changes in spinning gyroscopes whose rotors weighed 140 and 176 grams, or 5 and 6.3 ounces. When the gyroscopes were spun clockwise, as viewed from above, the researchers found no change in their weight. But when spun counterclockwise, they appeared to lose weight.[13]

30. It seems that children who spend more time watching popular programs on commercial television tend to be lower achievers in school. Several studies have established that performance on standardized tests varies in inverse proportion to the amount of television a child under the age of 12 watches. The more television of this sort a child watches, the lower his or her scores are likely to be.

31. Nostradamus, a 16th-century French physician, is said to have predicted with great accuracy things that occurred long after his death. His prophecies were written as short poems called quatrains. The following are said to foretell recent events:

> One burned, not dead, but apoplectical,
> Shall be found to have eaten up his hands,
> When the city shall damn the heretical man,
> Who as they thought had changed their laws.

> To the great empire, quite another shall come,
> Being distant from goodness and happiness,
> Governed by one of base parentage,
> The kingdom shall fall, a great unhappiness.

A prominent Nostrademus scholar interprets the first quatrain as referring to President Nixon's downfall and the Watergate scandal and the second as predicting the rise and dominance of communism and the subsequent subjugation of the Western democracies.[14]

32. From a flyer headed "Does Sunday School Make a Difference?":

Max Juken lived in New York. He did not believe in religious training. He refused to take his children to church, even when they asked to go. He has had 1062 descendants; 300 were sent to prison for an average term of 13 years; 190 were prostitutes; 680 were admitted alcoholics. His family, thus far, has cost the state in excess of $420,000. They made no contribution to society.

Jonathan Edwards lived in the same state, at the same time as the Jukens. He saw that his children were in church every Sunday. He had 929 descendants, of these 430 were ministers; 86 became college professors; 13 became university presidents; 75 authored good books; five were elected to the United States Congress, and two to the Senate. One was Vice-President of his nation. His family never cost the state one cent, but has contributed to the life of plenty in this land today.

33. A close friend is toying with the idea of becoming a scientologist, so I've decided to do some research on the Church of Scientology. I went to the library at the college where I work and found fifteen books in the library data base under the heading of "scientology." Six appeared to be critiques and exposes. But when I went to the shelves, I found all of the material critical of the Church to be missing and the librarian told me none of the books were checked out. It seems clear that somebody sympathetic to the Church has stolen (and probably destroyed) all material from the library collection that provides a negative picture of the Church. After further reflection, I'm convinced I must be right. This is just the sort of thing you would expect from a group of overzealous true believers.

34. Some dentists and alternative medical practitioners believe we are being poisoned by mercury contained in our dental fillings. They say that when we chew, minute quantities of mercury are released and ingested into the body, and that over time it is liable to reach toxic proportions. A flyer on mercury toxicity and dental fillings gives the following as symptoms related to mercury poisoning and suggests that if you have more than a few you ought to carefully consider having your mercury amalgam fillings removed:

Anxiety	Apathy
Confusion	Depression
Emotional instability	Fits of anger
Irritability	Nervousness

Nightmares	Tension
High blood pressure	Low blood pressure
Chronic headaches	Dizziness
Muscle twitches	Ringing in ears
Colds hands or feet	Decreased sexual activity
Leg cramps	Pain in joints
Weight loss	Fatigue
Drowsiness	Lack of energy
Allergies	Oversleeping
Bad breath	Bleeding gums
Acne	Rough skin
Skin flushes	Unexplained skin rashes

35. The following is from a popular advice column:

Dear Ann Landers: In a recent column, you recounted how *Reader's Digest* tested the honesty of Europeans by dropping wallets in various cities. You wondered how the United States would fare if put to the same test. Well, we can tell you. We did some U.S. testing and printed the results in the December 1995 issue. Here's a copy.

Lesta Cordil
Public Relations Associate Director, *Reader's Digest*

Dear Lesta: Many thanks for the assist. I'm sure my readers will find the results interesting. I certainly did. Readers, if you're wondering how your city stacked up (I thought Chicago would have done very well), you might not find the answer here. The experiment was done in only 12 cities. Here's how it was set up:

One hundred and twenty wallets containing $50 each were dropped on the streets and in the shopping malls, restaurants, gas stations and office buildings in a number of U.S. cities. In each wallet was a name, local address, phone number, family pictures and coupons, as well as the cash. A *Reader's Digest* reporter followed on the heels of the wallet-droppers, and this is what his research revealed.

Of the 120 wallets dropped, 80 were returned with all the money intact. Seattle turned out to be the most honest city. Nine of the ten wallets dropped in Seattle were returned with the $50 inside.

Three smaller cities turned out to be very near the top for honesty: Meadville, Pa.; Concord, N.H.; and Cheyenne, Wyo. In each of these cities eight wallets were returned and two were not.

St. Louis came in next—of the ten wallets dropped, seven were returned and three were kept. The suburbs of Boston tied with St. Louis. The suburbs of Los Angeles were not quite as honest. Six wallets were returned, four were kept. Four cities—Las Vegas; Dayton, Ohio; Atlanta; and the suburbs of Houston—shared the poorest records. Five wallets were returned and five were kept.

Small towns scored 80 percent returns and proved to be more honest than larger cities, with the exception of Seattle. Women, it turned out, were more honest than men—72 percent to 62 percent. Young people posted a 67 percent return rate—the same as the overall average.[15]

■
___

A Solution to Exercise I

The suggestion in this passage is that there is some sort of causal connection between an interest in science and an interest in music. The facts about Einstein and Newton are most likely meant to imply a correlation between the two, though the passage does not come right out and say that more scientists than nonscientists are interested in music. Otherwise there would be no reason to believe that a child's interest in music would lead him or her to pursue a career in science rather than something else. Now, even if such a correlation could be established serious questions could be raised about its significance. There are a number of ways of explaining such a correlation short of suggesting that an interest in music causes one to become interested in a career in science.

The real problem is that the passage involves the fallacy of omitting facts. We are told of two instances of well-known scientists showing an interest in music. But what about scientists generally? Do we have any reason to believe that what is true about Einstein and Newton is true of scientists generally or of more scientists than nonscientists? Lacking this information, the causal claim is wholly unfounded.

Notes

1. For an excellent account of the history of phlogiston theory and discussion of its philosophical implications, see *The Theory of Science: An Introduction to the History, Logic and Philosophy of Science,* by George Gale (New York: McGraw-Hill, 1979). I am indebted to Gale for the discussion of phlogiston in the text.

2. This is not to say that mainstream scientists do not on occasion engage in fallacious reasoning or worse. For more on this topic see *Betrayers of Truth: Fraud and Deceit in Science* by Broad and Wade (London: Oxford University Press, 1982).

3. For a detailed explanation of the curious events in the Bermuda triangle, see *The Bermuda Triangle Mystery — Solved* by Lawrence Kusche (New York: Warner, 1975).

4. Moody, Raymond A. *Life After Life*. New York: Bantam, 1975, pp. 21–22.

5. Have I violated Ockham's razor in claiming that invisible imps are as likely, all things being equal, as telepathy? Perhaps. But then again perhaps not. Are there good reasons to suppose that telepathy is any less bizarre than invisible imps?

6. This phrase was coined by John Stuart Mill (1806-1873) in *A System of Logic,* one of the first comprehensive studies on the ways causal connections are established.

7. The National Science Foundation reports that out of about 18,000 grants made in 1991, only 52 cases of misconduct were reported. On a more distressing note, however, a survey done that year by the National Association for the Advancement of Science of 1500 scientists revealed that more than a quarter of the respondents said they had witnessed faking, falsifying, or outright theft of research in the past decade.

8. For a good review of the controversy surrounding the work of Duesberg and Root-Bernstein see "Special Section—The AIDS Heresies," *Skeptic,* 1995, 3(2).

9. Medawar, P. B. *The Limits of Science.* New York: Harper and Row, 1984, p. 87.

10. Rivers, Donald. "First Photo of a Human Soul." *Weekly World News,* Sept. 15, 1992. Reprinted by permission of the publisher.

11. Gittelson, Bernard. *Bio-Rhythm: A Personal Science.* New York: Warner, 1975, pp. 15–19.

12. Hayes, John. "Ex-OSU Professor Theorizes About Alien Beings." *Oregonian,* Jan. 18, 1987. Reprinted by permission of the author.

13. Copyright 1989 by the New York Times Company. Reprinted by permission. This experiment was replicated a year and a half later by two physicists at Tokyo University. See Imanishi, A., Marayuma, K., Midorikawa, S., and Morimote, T. "Observation Against the Weight Reduction in Spinning Gyroscopes." *Journal of the Physical Society of Japan,* Apr. 1991, 60(4). They detected no weight change due to the rotation of their gyroscopes. Since then no further reports of research on this phenomenon have surfaced in the scientific literature. Do you sense a conspiracy here?

14. Adapted from Roberts, Henry C. (trans., ed.) *The Complete Prophesies of Nostradamus.* New York: Nostradamus Co., 1982.

15. "Dear Ann Landers." *Oregonian,* Nov. 24, 1996.

Further Reading

Scientific Method and the Philosophy of Science

Elster, Jon. *Nuts and Bolts for the Social Sciences*. Cambridge: Cambridge University Press, 1989.

Gale, George. *Theory of Science: An Introduction to the History, Logic and Philosophy of Science*. New York: McGraw-Hill, 1979.

Giere, Ronald N. *Understanding Scientific Reasoning*. (3rd ed.) New York: Holt, Rinehart and Winston, 1991.

Hacking, Ian. *Representing and Intervening: Introductory Topics in the Philosophy of Natural Science*. Cambridge: Cambridge University Press, 1983.

Hempel, Carl G. *The Philosophy of Natural Science*. Englewood Cliffs, N.J.: Prentice-Hall, 1966.

Homans, George C. *The Nature of a Social Science*. New York: Harcourt, Brace & World, 1967.

Huck, Schuyler W., and Sandler, Howard M. *Rival Hypotheses: Alternative Interpretations of Data Based Conclusions*. New York: Harper and Row, 1979.

Kuhn, Thomas S. *The Structure of Scientific Revolutions*. (2nd ed.) Chicago: University of Chicago Press, 1970.

Medawar, P. B. *The Limits of Science*. New York: Harper and Row, 1984.

Moore, Kathleen Dean. *A Field Guide to Inductive Arguments*. (2nd ed.) Dubuque: Kendall/Hunt, 1989.

Popper, Karl R. *The Logic of Scientific Discovery*. (2nd rev. ed.) New York: Harper Torchbooks, 1968.

Salmon, Merrilee H., and others. *Introduction to the Philosophy of Science*. Englewood Cliffs, N.J.: Prentice-Hall, 1992.

Toulmin, Stephen. *The Philosophy of Science: An Introduction*. New York: Harper and Row, 1960.

Pseudoscience

Abell, G. O., and Singer, B. *Science and the Paranormal*. New York: Scribner, 1981.

Broad, William, and Wade, Nicholas. *Betrayers of the Truth: Fraud and Deceit in Science*. Oxford: Oxford University Press, 1982.

Gardner, Martin. *Fads and Fallacies in the Name of Science*. New York: Dover, 1957.

Gardner, Martin. *Science: Good, Bad and Bogus*. Buffalo, N.Y.: Prometheus, 1981.

Glymour, Clark, and Stalker, Douglas. *Examining Holistic Medicine*. Buffalo, N.Y.: Prometheus, 1985.

Gray, William D. *Thinking Critically About the New Age*. Belmont, Calif.: Wadsworth, 1991.

Hines, Terence. *Pseudo-Science and the Paranormal*. Buffalo, N.Y.: Prometheus, 1988.

Hyman, Ray. *The Elusive Quarry: A Scientific Appraisal of Psychical Research*. Buffalo, N.Y.: Prometheus, 1989.

National Council Against Health Fraud Newsletter, Box 1276, Loma Linda, Calif., 92354.

Radner, Daisie, and Radner, Michael. *Science and Unreason*. Belmont, Calif.: Wadsworth, 1982.

Randi, James, *Flim-Flam! The Truth about Unicorns, Parapsychology and Other Delusions*. New York: Thomas Y. Crowell, 1980.

Sagan, Carl. *The Demon-Haunted World: Science as a Candle in the Dark*. New York: Random House, 1996.

Shultz, Ted. (ed.) *The Fringes of Reason: A Whole Earth Catalogue*. New York: Harmony, 1989.

Skeptic Magazine, P.O. Box 338, Altadena, Calif., 91001.

Skeptical Inquirer, Box 229, Buffalo, N.Y., 14215-0229.

Index